Physician's Guide
*Evaluating Employment Opportunities
and Avoiding Contractual Pitfalls*

Physician's Guide

Evaluating Employment Opportunities and Avoiding Contractual Pitfalls

Thomas C. Crawford

Copyright © 2011 by Thomas C. Crawford.

Mill City Press, Inc.
212 3rd Avenue North, Suite 290
Minneapolis, MN 55401
612.455.2294
www.millcitypublishing.com

All rights reserved. No part of this publication may be reproduced, stored in a retrieval system, or transmitted, in any form or by any means, electronic, mechanical, photocopying, recording, or otherwise, without the prior written permission of the author.

ISBN-13: 978-1-936780-23-5
LCCN: 2011925057

Cover Design and Typeset by Wendy Baker

Printed in the United States of America

Author's Note

Thomas C. Crawford, MBA, FACHE

Correspondence concerning this guide should be addressed to
Thomas C. Crawford, 11180 NW 20th Ave, Gainesville, FL 32606.
thomascrawford@consultant.com

Table of Contents

Introduction ix

Evaluating Employment Opportunities
    Chapter 1: Before the Search 3
    Chapter 2: Job Search Resources 7
    Chapter 3: The Spirit of the Agreement 11
    Chapter 4: Evaluating Culture 15
    Chapter 5: Medical Staff Bylaws and Rules and Regulations
    of the Medical Staff 23

Avoiding Contractual Pitfalls
    Chapter 6: How Will Your Pay Be Calculated 27
    Chapter 7: Patient Volume and the Pro Forma 39
    Chapter 8: Malpractice Insurance 47
    Chapter 9: Call Expectations 51
    Chapter 10: Free Money = Time Commitment 57
    Chapter 11: Termination Covenants 63
    Chapter 12: Non-Compete Covenants 69
    Chapter 13: Miscellaneous Contractual Pitfalls 75
    Chapter 14: Interviewing Checklist 79
    Chapter 15: Contracting Checklist 83

Epilogue 87

About the Author 89

References 91

Introduction

On April 21, 2010, I gave a grand rounds lecture titled, "The Business of Medicine: Evaluating Employment Opportunities and Avoiding Contractual Pitfalls" to 40 resident physicians. Throughout the presentation, I highlighted common contractual pitfalls, provided attendees with tools for evaluating their potential employers, and helped attendees prepare for ensuring recruiting promises are contractually obligated. The presentation went well—the group was engaged, no post-call resident went to sleep, and I was delighted with the depth of the questions. However, while picking up my presentation materials, a graduating resident came forward with a look of grave concern on his face. He asked me the following question: "Where were you three months ago?"

During the course of my 17-year healthcare career, I've been privileged to meet and work with many talented physicians of all specialties. I've witnessed firsthand their unwavering dedication to their medical communities, and I've seen patients benefit from the physicians' years of training. Nevertheless, I've always found it ironic that world-class athletes with considerably less education always sought industry-specific representation when turning professional and, conversely, graduating resident physicians who successfully completed four years of undergraduate studies, four years of medical school, up to six years of residency, and potentially two years of fellowship were diving headlong into the business realities of employment selection and contracting relatively unassisted.

As a senior healthcare executive in the positions of chief executive officer (CEO) and chief operating officer (COO), I've interviewed hundreds of physicians and, regrettably, I've seen the aftermath of unfulfilled recruiting promises as a result of situations including bankruptcy due to a lack of volume, unsustainable call, terminations without cause, and questionable business practices.

Each case study provided within this guide is based on circumstances relayed to me by physicians during the interview process (specialties and locations have been changed to ensure anonymity).

Throughout my career, I've helped a relatively small number of physicians out of their untoward circumstances; however, a vast majority of the physicians were contractually bound to unacceptable covenants they simply did not read or comprehend. Thus, the premise for this guide is to provide resident physicians and early careerists with the basic tools required for evaluating employment opportunities and transforming recruiting promises into contractual covenants.

The brevity of this guide is to ensure it is an "easy read," which can be readily referenced when needed. Utilize the tools provided in this guide, and always seek industry-specific representation before signing a contract so you can eliminate or mitigate all unnecessary and unwanted professional and personal "disruptions."

Evaluating Employment Opportunities

Chapter 1
Before the Search

You are a scarce commodity. This simplistic assertion was captured quantitatively by Dill and Salsberg (2008), when they forecasted a chasm (see Figure 1) between the current and future quantity of physicians (all specialties) and the growing aggregate demand for healthcare services, and noted that it widens as the Baby Boom demographic continues to age and consumes an unprecedented amount of the healthcare resources.

Additionally, the current physician shortage has become glaringly evident in primary care, leading the U.S. Department of Health and Human Services – Health Resources and Services Administration (HRSA) to designate Health Professional Shortage Areas (HPSA) and create various federal incentives, such as grants and discounted pharmaceuticals, for practicing within these identified communities. The following data highlights the magnitude of the current dilemma:

"As of September 30, 2009, there were:

6,204 Primary Care HPSAs with 65 million people living in them. It would take 16,643 practitioners to meet their need for primary care providers (a population to practitioner ratio of 2,000:1).

3,291 Mental Health HPSAs with 80 million people living in them. It would take 5,338 practitioners to meet their need for mental health providers (a population to practitioner ratio of 10,000:1)" (HRSA, 2010, "Health Professional Shortage Areas").

The national shortage of physicians (manifesting in intense recruitment, growing underserved areas, and federal interventions) will deepen over the next 15 years. Nevertheless, understanding that you are a scarce commodity and creating a realistic opportunity to capitalize on this fact is completely up to you.

Before searching for your next position, it is imperative that you and, if applicable, your significant other, create a single ascending list of personal and professional priorities. In healthcare, you cannot have a professional priority that does not affect your personal life and vice versa. For example, call coverage (emergency department and practice) will affect the time you have available for your family, and the local hospital's medical staff bylaws may determine where you can live and, consequently, where you send your kids to school. With this stated, your list will also help you formulate interview questions (think in terms of call coverage requirements, loan forgiveness, sign-on bonus, and geographic restrictions).

The ascending list of priorities will crystallize your search criteria and will help you filter out numerous positions; however, it is always important to realize that if a particular geographic location is your number-one priority, you may inadvertently sacrifice a preponderance of your negotiating leverage for that specific location (meaning you assume more risk). For example, if your top priority is to be in Orlando, Florida and your number-two priority is to offset your medical school debt through loan forgiveness, it is very unlikely that you will receive loan forgiveness in an area dominated by a for-profit health system and saturated with physicians who are competing in private practices. This paradigm is referred to as the *location reality check*. Are you willing to potentially sacrifice your negotiating leverage for the perfect location? The answer will be captured within your ascending list of priorities.

Recommendation

- Create an ascending list of personal and professional priorities to refine your search criteria and establish your interview questions.

Figure 1

Baseline Physician FTE Supply and Demand Projections, 2006-2025

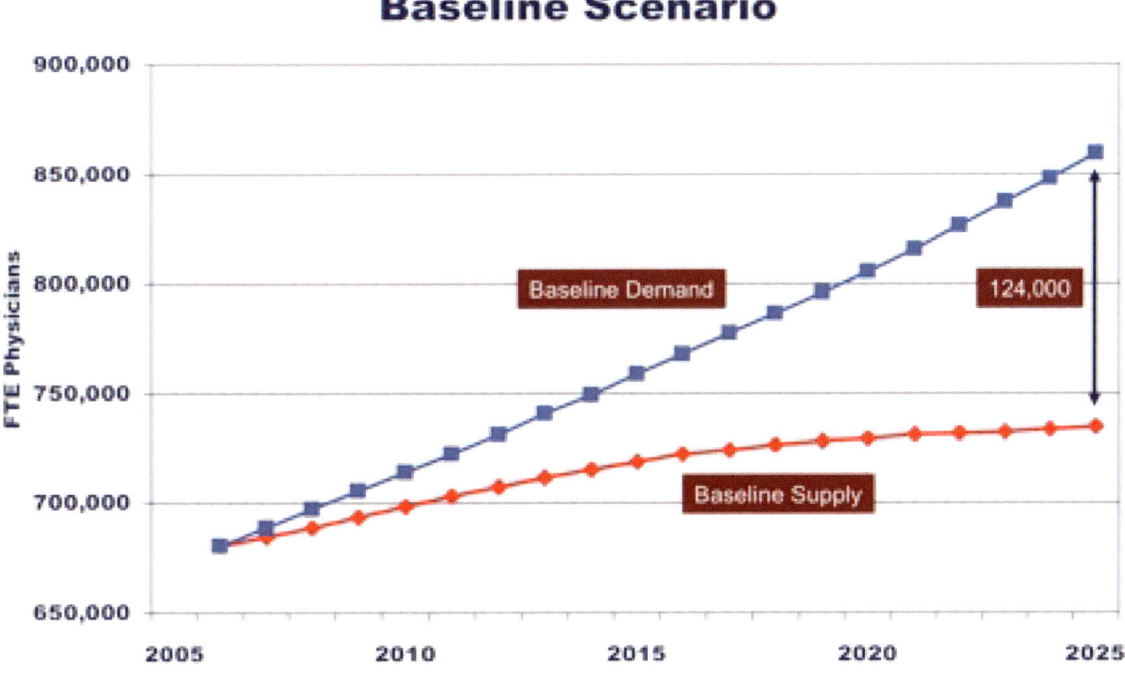

Figure 1. Baseline Physician FTE Supply and Demand Projections, 2006-2025. Reprinted from Dill, M.J. & Salsberg, E.S. (2008). The Complexities of Physician Supply and Demand: Projections Through 2025. Association of American Medical Colleges: Washington, D.C. Reprinted with permission.

Chapter 2
Job Search Resources

Table 1 lists job boards, and Table 2 lists physician recruiters/search firms. Each table is organized by URL (uniform resource locator), and each resource is readily accessible via the Internet. With this stated, once you've entered your personal data, you may have your curriculum vitae circulated to, or retrieved by, employers around the country. To ensure you do not become inundated with phone calls and e-mails at work and at home, consider creating a new Gmail, Yahoo, or other web-based e-mail account specifically for the purpose of managing replies from recruiters, search firms, and potential employers.

Additional Resources

The American Medical Association website (ama-assoc.org) provides information and resources for young careerists. This site also provides a comprehensive listing of the medical specialty colleges and associations, and a preponderance of the association sites offer navigable job boards.

Recommendations

- Use the resources outlined in Table 1 and Table 2 to help locate employment opportunities.
- When posting your curriculum vitae, consider creating a new web-based e-mail account to manage replies from recruiters/potential employers.

Table 1
Job Boards

Company/Organization	Website URL	Notes
AllHealthCareJobs	allhealthcarejobs.com	All Specialties
American College of Physicians	acponline.com	Internal Medicine and Family Physician
American Association of Medical Colleges	aamc.org/careerconnect/start.htm	All Specialties
American Academy of Family Physicians	www.aafp.org/careerads/	Family Physician
Journal of the American Medical Association	jamacareernet.ama-assn.org	All Specialties
MDSearch	mdsearch.com	All Specialties
MedCenter Today	medcentertoday.com/jobs.php	Academic Postings All Specialties
Medical Workers	medicalworkers.com	All Specialties
MomMD	mommd.com	All Specialties for Women in Medicine
National Association of Physician Recruiters	napr.org	All Specialties
National Coalition of Health Care Recruiters	nchcr.com	All Specialties
New England Journal of Medicine	nejmjobs.com	All Specialties
onTargetjobs Company	medhunters.com	All Specialties - Locums and Permanent
Physician Depot	physiciandepot.com	All Specialties
Physician Work	physicianwork.com	All Specialties
PhysicianAndPractice	physicianandpractice.com	All Specialties
PhysicianCareerJobs	physiciancareerjobs.com	All Specialties
PhysicianCrossroads	physiciancrossroads.com	All Specialties
PhysicianEmployment.org, Inc.	physicianemployment.org	All Specialties
Physicians Employment	physemp.com	All Specialties

Company/Organization	Website URL	Notes
Practice Match	practicematch.com	All Specialties
PracticeLink, Ltd.	practicelink.com	All Specialties

Table 2
Physician Recruiters

Company/Organization	Website URL	Notes
Association of Staff Physician Recruiters	aspr.org	Browse "In-House" Recruiters by State
Canadian Association of Staff Physician Recruiters	caspr.org	Browse Canadian "In-House" Recruiters by City
National Association of Physician Recruiters	napr.org	Browse Member Search Firms by State
Northeast Physician Recruiters Association	nepra.org	Browse Northeast Recruiters by State
Southwest Physician Recruiters Association	swpra.org	Browse Southwest Recruiters by State

Chapter 3
The Spirit of the Agreement

Bagley (2002) defines a contract as "a legally enforceable promise or set of promises." (G-5, Glossary). The definition is simplistic; however, it provides the perfect opportunity to highlight and underscore a fundamental and vitally important takeaway from this guide: If it isn't written down, it doesn't exist. You cannot rely on anecdotal comments made during the recruitment process or stated in the contractual covenants that are not clearly defined.

To illustrate this salient point, please consider the following two hypothetical examples (one from an academic institution, and one from a community hospital).

Example 1

An internal medicine physician scientist accepts a position with a leading academic university and is provided with $300,000 of commitment capital for three years ($100,000 per year) and a mission effort that is 60% clinical and 40% research. The physician scientist applies for numerous grants and, understanding the competitiveness of the grant funding process, uses the start-up capital judiciously during the first three years. At the end of the commitment period, the physician scientist has $175,000 in commitment capital that has not been utilized, as well as a number of pending grants. Will the physician scientist be able to spend the remaining $175,000 in commitment capital to maintain his current mission effort? The assumption might be yes; however, the chair of the medicine department will determine the answer. Why? Simply because it was not discussed, agreed to, and captured contractually.

Example 2

A general surgeon accepts an employed position with a community hospital for less than the national median compensation for the surgeon's specialty. However, the hospital demonstrates that the market potential is excellent, and the contract states that the general surgeon will be entitled to the net income, less overhead/expenses, that the practice produces. The general surgeon works diligently to build the referral streams necessary to support the practice during the first year of employment and despite best efforts, the practice loses $75,000 in its first year. Nevertheless, the general surgeon's unwavering effort is rewarded with additional patient volume during the second year, and the practice generates a net profit of $50,000. Is the general surgeon entitled to the $50,000 in net profit or, conversely, can the hospital claim the practice is still posting a loss of $25,000 after two years? After working tirelessly for two years to establish a practice, while being paid less than the national median, the assumption might be that the general surgeon is entitled to the $50,000. However, the hospital's CEO or designee will determine the decision. Why? Again, because it was not discussed, agreed to, and captured contractually.

You need to think of your employment contract in the same context as a prenuptial agreement—the time to work through the details is when the relationship is strongest and before it is consummated. You can take nothing for granted, and nothing can be assumed or implied. Therefore, the contract should be as granular as possible to ensure it is easily interpreted and reflects the spirit in which you're signing it. An easily interpreted contract will ensure that you fully comprehend your employment situation, will help prevent the causes that produce voluntary turnover, and will limit disruptions to your career and personal life.

The reasons for voluntary physician turnover are reflected in the results of a 2006 Retention Survey from the American Medical Group Association (AMGA) and Cejka Search (Cejka Search, 2009, "Key Findings"), which highlight the following:

- 51% leave due to a "poor cultural fit."
  - Refer to Chapter 4 for cultural assessment tools.
- 42% leave "to be closer to own or spouse's family."

- Refer to Chapter 1 (ascending list of personal and professional priorities).
- 32% leave to "seek higher compensation."
  - Refer to Chapters 3, 6, and 7.
- 22% leave because "spouse's job required relocation."
- This is acceptable turnover; meaning, it is difficult to forecast and avoid.
- 20% leave to find a "better community fit."
  - Refer to Chapter 4 for community assessment tools.
- 17% leave due to an "incompatible work schedule."
  - Refer to Chapters 3 and 9.
- 17% leave due to an "excessive call schedule."
  - Refer to Chapters 3 and 9.

Reprinted from the AMGA and Cejka Search 2006 Physician Retention Survey, American Medical Group Association (www.amga.org). Reprinted with permission.

The AMGA Retention Survey also highlights that 12% of physicians left within one year of starting employment. If this number is extrapolated against the total estimated number of physicians, the systemic consequence of physicians not being prepared to evaluate culture or negotiate employment contracts begins to manifest. Consider the following:

- 700,000 physicians x 6.7% turnover rate = 46,900 physicians leaving annually.
- 46,900 physicians x 12% = 5,228 physicians leaving their positions within 12 months.
- 5228 physicians / 260 business days = 21.6 physicians.

PHYSICIAN'S GUIDE: EVALUATING EMPLOYMENT OPPORTUNITIES AND AVOIDING CONTRACTUAL PITFALLS

Essentially, an estimated 22 physicians per day are handing in their resignations within the first 12 months of employment.

Three of the top seven reasons for voluntary physician turnover (compensation, work schedule, and call schedule) could be mitigated, if not eliminated, during the recruiting (interview), negotiating, and contracting processes.

During the interview, you will be armed with your interview questions, produced by your ascending list of personal and professional priorities, and you will also need to take notes, writing down every response to every question you ask. Additionally, you need to capture every recruiting promise made to you during the interview process by each member of the interview team (this is the "spirit" in which you are deciding to accept an employment position). Once you receive your letter of offer or employment contract, you simply contrast the document against the answers to your questions and the recruiting promises. If you cannot find the answers/promises within the contractual covenants, you need to add the language. If you locate the language within the contract and find it ambiguous, you need to add granular verbiage to ensure the covenant is easily interpreted. To illustrate this point, consider the following:

When I was the CEO of a health system, I interviewed and hired a number of employed physicians for my medical staff, and I honored the contractual covenants and the spirit of each agreement. Be that as it may, my career evolved down an academic track, and I made the difficult decision to leave my health system. Now, the contracts of the employed physicians I recruited and hired are subject to interpretation by a new CEO, who was not present during the recruiting, negotiating, and contracting processes.

Finally, please understand that even the most seasoned healthcare lawyers are not going to bring contractual shortfalls to your attention if they are unaware of the recruitment promises made to you.

Recommendations

- Take notes during the interview/recruitment process to capture the answers to your questions and the recruitment promises made to you.

- Use the list of answers/promises to contrast against your employment contract and ensure that each answer/promise is reflected within the contract with easily interpreted language.

Chapter 4
Evaluating Culture

You will not be able to determine the culture of an organization during an interview or through touring a facility and randomly meeting its employees; with this stated, this chapter was designed to provide you with the analytical tools required to determine if you are the right fit prior to accepting a position.

As previously referenced, poor cultural fit (Cejka Search, 2009, "Key Findings") was the leading cause of voluntary physician turnover and, consequently, is the premise behind this chapter. However, before providing cultural assessment tools, an operational definition for healthcare workplace culture is required.

Culture is defined as "the behaviors and beliefs characteristic of a particular social, ethnic, or age group" (Culture, 2010). With this stated, our working definition for healthcare culture will be: The opinions and behaviors that influence the workplace environment.

The established healthcare culture definition will be applied to the following cultural stratums which, depending on the size of your employer, will directly affect your job satisfaction:

- Micro-Culture: Your practice, clinic, division, or immediate work environment.

- Medial-Culture: Hospital, medical staff, department, or large multi-specialty group practice.

- Macro-Culture: College, university, health consortium, or health system.

- External-Culture: Town, city, or county.

Why is it difficult to assess culture during the interview process? Because, quite simply, you are seeing employees, potential colleagues, and members of leadership at their best and, by design, you may not be exposed to anyone who is unable to "sell" the employment opportunity. Although I cannot speak for other CEOs, I will tell you truthfully that when I had a physician candidate interview at my hospital, I personally coordinated the facility tour and meet-and-greet events down to a granular level. I tried to ensure that the candidate did not tour specific departments of my hospital where employees or physicians working in those areas were unhappy, for any reason, with their colleagues or my organization. It was my overriding objective to make sure all candidates had pleasant interview processes and were not exposed to any individual I considered to be a malcontent. If a physician, during the tour, the luncheon, or the recruitment dinner, stated anything that was less than positive, I simply made sure that person was not present during the interview process for the next candidate.

A first and second interview generally lasts no longer than a combined total of four days; therefore, there is a limited window of opportunity to evaluate the cultures with which you will be working. It is essential that you know which questions to ask, why the questions are important, and how the answers will influence your job satisfaction. To ensure that you are equipped with an armamentarium of cultural assessment tools, the following questions in Table 3, Table 4, Table 5, and Table 6 were designed, by stratum, to ensure you fully comprehend the cultural contexts of potential employers. Many of the questions for the medial-cultural (Table 4) and macro-cultural (Table 5) assessments are synonymous; therefore, these tables contain new questions or the same questions with different perspectives regarding the importance or the potential influence on your job satisfaction.

Finally, do not be apprehensive about assessing the cultures in which you will be working. The most thorough interview I conducted was with a family practice physician from Connecticut, who, on her second visit, brought a nurse manager along from a hospital to which she admitted patients. The nurse manager interviewed the nurses and physicians working on the medical/surgical and intensive care units. During the interview process, the nurse manager was able to assess the medial-culture of her colleague's employment opportunity by asking questions about medical staff; nursing and employee morale; patient safety indicators and satisfaction; and the strategic direction and core values of the organization. With a solid understanding of the hospital's culture, the family practice physician decided to accept the employment offer and, as of 2010, is still employed by the organization five years later.

Recommendations

- Use the micro, medial, macro, and external cultural assessment questions to determine if you will be the right "fit" for an employment opportunity.

- If you have questions about an institutional culture, contact your predecessor, previous employees, or current employees.

Table 3
Micro-Cultural Assessment

Question	Importance	Potential Impact
Is physician satisfaction measured and what, if applicable, is the frequency of measurement? **If yes, request a copy of the results.**	Physician satisfaction measurement provides practice leadership with an opportunity to understand what is working well and what is detracting or dissatisfying the physicians within a practice. This should be measured at least biennially.	If physician satisfaction isn't measured, you need to understand how you will provide feedback on any practice element you find dissatisfying (example: Staff meetings). Additionally, you run the risk of losing colleagues, which will affect the financial performance of the practice and potentially your call expectations.
Is employee satisfaction measured and what, if applicable, is the frequency of measurement? **If yes, request a copy of the results.**	Employee satisfaction measurement, depending on the size of the practice, provides the leadership with an opportunity to understand if employees perceive their treatment as fair, and it provides an opportunity to understand the job elements that are dissatisfying. This should be measured at least annually.	Nothing will disrupt a practice quicker than turnover because industry specific knowledge is acquired through training and experience, and practice-specific knowledge, mainly physician preferences, can only be acquired through provider-specific exposure.
Is patient satisfaction measured and what, if applicable, is the frequency of measurement?	High patient satisfaction is the hallmark of a successful practice and should be measured at least quarterly.	If you are joining a practice where patient satisfaction is high, you will immediately enjoy success by association; however, if the satisfaction is low, your reputation will suffer by association.
How tenured are the physicians?	If physician satisfaction is not measured, tenure is a good indication of satisfaction (based on the premise that unhappy physicians are less likely to remain in environments with which they are not satisfied).	As stated under physician satisfaction with the following caveat: You need to ensure tenured physicians are amenable to listening to suggestions for change so that you do not have to compromise your style of practice.
How tenured are the employees?	If employee satisfaction is not measured, tenure is a good indication of satisfaction.	Again, you need to ensure that the staff is amenable to suggestions for change.
Would the physicians and employees be receptive to suggestions for changes in processes?	Not fitting into a culture generally is a result of the behaviors not matching a physician's desired	If physicians and employees are not amenable to change, you may be entering a practice that is too rigid and may result in

Question	Importance	Potential Impact
	performance.	your continually molding your practice style and values to that of the group.
Why, if applicable, did your predecessor leave? **Ask if you may have his/her contact information.**	To ensure you are not walking into a less-than-desirable employment opportunity, you need to speak to your predecessor (make sure to capture the facts versus fixating on opinions).	Unfortunately, the old adage holds true: Unless we learn from history, we're doomed to repeat it, and you don't want to find yourself in a situation that could have been prevented prior to commencing practice (examples: Rude employee, inflexible physician).
What is the financial health of the practice? **Request a copy of the financials (balance sheet, income statement, and statement of cash flows).**	Nothing changes a business culture faster than financial challenges.	Joining a financially challenged practice can affect your pay, your work schedule, and the resources available to you.

Table 4
Medial-Cultural Assessment

Question	Importance	Potential Impact
Is medical staff satisfaction measured and what, if applicable, is the frequency of measurement? **If yes, request a copy of the results, and ask how items of concern are actively addressed.**	Medical staff satisfaction measurement provides an indication of the pros and cons of practicing within a hospital or large multi-disciplinary department and should be measured at least biennially.	If medical staff satisfaction isn't measured, you need to understand how to communicate issues to the leadership, as well as the process for problem resolution. Additionally, the hospital or department leadership should clearly define appropriate lines for communication and detail their retention strategy.
Is nursing satisfaction measured and what, if applicable, is the frequency of measurement? **If yes, request a copy of the results.**	Nursing satisfaction measurement is imperative because it will affect your quality of life and, potentially, the quality of the care you provide. This should be measured at least annually	Unseasoned nurses can dramatically increase the number of times you are interrupted during office hours, the frequency of after-hours calls, and the quality of the care you deliver (examples: Decubitus ulcer, patient falls, failure to rescue).
Is institutional and/or departmental quality of care measured, and against what peer group will you be benchmarked? **Request a copy of the results.**	At a minimum, the institution should be able to provide you with data on Core Measures, nursing-specific indicators, and mortality. If the data is not readily available, this should be a red flag (quality is paramount and is the foundation of all healthcare payment reform discussions).	Similar to patient satisfaction, you immediately enjoy success by association; however, if the quality is low, your reputation will suffer by association.
What are the core values of the institution/department?	If the core values are written or can be articulated, it is important to ensure they do not conflict with your professional beliefs.	You want to avoid professional conflict. For example, you may believe in a culture of safety, and the primary core value of an institution could be financial health. This could potentially produce a conflict.
What is the strategic direction of the institution/department?	This will let you know what is important to the organization. Essentially, in what is the institution/department investing?	Again, you want to ensure the direction does not conflict with your practice, beliefs, and values.
How tenured is the leadership?	Nothing will disrupt a culture faster than a change in leadership.	New leaders bring a fresh perspective and a new agenda. Essentially, they are the

Table 4
Medial-Cultural Assessment

Question	Importance	Potential Impact
		catalysts for change, and this will influence (good or bad) the institutional culture.

Table 5
Macro-Cultural Assessment

Question	Importance	Potential Impact
What is the financial health of the university or system? **Request a copy of the financials (balance sheet, income statement, and statement of cash flows).**	No circumstances will invade the medial- and micro-cultures faster than financial challenges.	Joining a financially challenged university or system will dramatically affect the culture and potentially the resources available to you on both the micro and medial levels.

Table 6
External-Cultural Assessment

Question	Importance	Potential Impact
Is the local economy strong, or is it weak?	A faltering local economy will mean less jobs and a less favorable payer mix (patients with insurance).	You could end up providing a disproportionate amount of uncompensated care, which will influence the bottom line of your practice and, potentially, your compensation.
How strong is the local school system? Is there a private school within commuting distance?	If you currently have children, you need to interview school personnel before accepting a job. If you are thinking about having children, you need to know the quality of the educational system.	Depending on the medical staff bylaws (see Chapter 5), you may not be able to move to another town with a better public school system; thus, leaving you with the following three options: • Send your child to a poorly performing school system. • Pay tuition and commute to a more favorable school. • Leave your place of employment.

Chapter 5

Medical Staff Bylaws and Rules and Regulations of the Medical Staff

If your employment is contingent upon being able to admit, treat, or operate on patients within a hospital setting, you need to review the hospital's medical staff bylaws and the rules and regulations of the medical staff. The bylaws serve as the formal self-governance structure of the physicians and, if applicable, other licensed and credentialed providers, such as psychologists and dentists, as delegated by the board of trustees. The rules and regulations outline institutional policies and protocols, such as admitting and emergency room processes; records and charting; and laboratory service orders. Sequentially, you should review the bylaws before accepting an employment opportunity, and you need to review the rules and regulations prior to treating a patient within the hospital.

Beyond the governance structure, including officers and committee responsibilities, the bylaws outline the following items that may affect your job satisfaction or, potentially, your employment status:

- Qualifications for membership and privileges.

- Decision-making methods and conflict resolution.

- Investigations, corrective action plans, and hearing and appeal plans.

- Emergency corrective action.

- Automatic suspension and termination.

- Hearing and appeal processes.

- Final decisions by the board of trustees.

- Meeting attendance requirements.

When reading the medical staff bylaws and rules and regulations, do not skim through the document. Be sure to pay attention to any item that may directly influence you now or in the future.

Example of medical staff bylaws

The following vignette is commonly found in a hospital's bylaws:

Affiliate and/or Active Staff shall live and maintain an office in _____ County.

This covenant underscores the necessity of reviewing the bylaws and conducting an external cultural assessment prior to accepting an employment offer. Essentially, if you want to move to another county, yet continue your employment at your current practice or hospital, you could have your hospital privileges revoked or non-renewed based on your place of residence. This is because you would be unable to admit, operate, or treat your patients within the hospital setting, and this typically will result in a termination or voluntary resignation if the conflict is not quickly remedied.

Example of rules and regulations of the medical staff

The following rule is prevalent in institutions throughout the United States:

"Adherence – in the event a physician does not comply with these Rules and Regulations, the Chief Executive Officer, or his/her designee, will discontinue the operating/admitting privileges of this physician except in Emergencies."

What does this mean? I had a similar rule at my hospital, and the institutional interpretation was as follows: If you were not in compliance with something (re-credentialing paperwork or medical records were incomplete, for example), your hospital privileges would be administratively suspended; however, you were still expected to take an equitable share of emergency department call ("except in emergencies"). If you were in a private practice, your ability to generate income would be significantly limited, or if you were employed by the hospital, your paycheck could be reduced or withheld, even though you continued to provide equitable call coverage.

The medical staff bylaws and the rules and regulations of the medical staff should be provided to you upon request. Although there are minor nuances from institution to institution, you will find that both documents have similar frameworks for content, regardless of location.

Recommendations

- Review the medical staff bylaws before accepting an employment offer.
- Review the rules and regulations of the medical staff prior to commencing employment.

Avoiding Contractual Pitfalls

Chapter 6
How Will Your Pay Be Calculated

Thirty-two percent of physicians "leave to seek higher compensation" (Cejka Search, 2009, "Key Findings"). Unfortunately, resident physicians and early careerists routinely enter into contractual arrangements based on the good faith produced during the recruitment process. Nevertheless, a lack of remuneration comprehension could significantly affect a physician's expected compensation immediately upon employment or in the near future.

From multi-specialty groups, to partnerships, to hospitals, the physician shortage has created a countless quantity of employment opportunities and compensation models. To ensure adequate access and tolerable call coverage, while mitigating any financial burden born by the employer, creative compensation models have been developed.

What follows are the most prevalent compensation models, their advantages, and the associated financial dangers of which you should be aware. Note: The nomenclature may change from location to location; nevertheless, the premise and the highlighted potential hazards remain consistent.

Employed Model

A straight employment model mitigates the risks associated with the other models by ensuring that the contracted salary is guaranteed; nevertheless, depending on the term (evergreen versus a defined period of time), there are two potential pitfalls of which to be aware.

An evergreen employment contract has no end date, which means the contract remains in effect until either party terminates it, for cause or without cause. One of the keys to negotiating an evergreen contract is to ensure that cost of living raises

(COLA) are contractually obligated by the employer. For example, members of a medical staff negotiated competitive employment model contracts for themselves, and they willfully executed their evergreen contracts. Unfortunately, their contracts did not include any reference to COLA adjustments, and when the new CEO was appointed at the hospital, he had several members of the medical staff who had not received raises for the better part of a decade. A competitive contract negotiated in 1997 was well below median compensation for primary care providers (25th percentile) in 2007. The result was that some of the institution's mid-level managers, who were receiving annual COLA and merit salary increases, had higher annual salaries than the physicians working in the clinic, admitting patients, and taking call.

An employment contract with a defined period of time will guarantee salary over the course of the agreement and, like the evergreen contract, COLA adjustments and/or annual salary increases should be included. Nevertheless, you need to pay specific attention to the covenant for contract renewal and ensure that your ending salary will be the starting point for negotiating your next contract or you will, essentially, run the risk of having your salary reduced. Example: A pediatrician signs a three-year employment contract for $150,000 per year with a minimum guaranteed COLA increase of 3% per year. The pediatrician's practice grows steadily; however, due to a poor payer mix (mix of insurance, bad debt, and charity care), the group practice loses money on the pediatrician's practice during the course of the agreement. After the three years conclude, the executive director of the group practice begins the new contract negotiations with a base salary of $125,000, because the contract renewal language did not specify an auto-renew and/or guarantee that any subsequent contract would be based on the final year's base salary.

The advantage of the employment model is that it mitigates the risks assumed by the other models, and it guarantees a contractually defined salary during the life of the contract.

Net Revenue Model

Net revenue models provide a base salary, and a percentage of the net revenue (net receipts minus practice expenses) can be reconciled quarterly, semi-annually, or as an end-of-year bonus. On the surface, a net revenue model contract my appear to be an employment arrangement with an opportunity for a bonus, but you need to ensure that your base salary is competitive and ensure that you are fully aware of the indirect expenses that will be attributed to your practice and, consequently, will limit your income potential. For an example, refer to the internal medicine physician case study (Case Study 1) at the end of this chapter.

The advantage to the net revenue model is that it mirrors the concept of a private practice by rewarding physicians for their sweat equity by providing that all or a predefined share of the net revenue is given back to the physicians. To ensure this model works to your advantage, you need to fully comprehend the details behind the overhead that will be expensed against your practice.

Income Guarantee Model

Based on my experience, income guarantees possess the highest amount of financial risk of all compensation models because you essentially commence your practice on a loan. The loan allows you to draw a salary, pay for fringe benefits and, if applicable, offset practice operating costs while you begin seeing patients and generating revenue. Nevertheless, at the end of the income guarantee period (generally one to two years), if you have not offset/repaid the loan dollars you have utilized, you will find yourself in debt and in the position of lowering your salary to cover your practice costs and the unpaid portion of the loan. In some instances, the unpaid portion of the loan will be forgiven over time (see Chapter 10 on Free Money = Time Commitment); however, if you decide, for any reason, to leave your practice before the end of the forgiveness period, you will owe a prorated portion of the loan plus interest. Example: A dermatologist accepts an income guarantee of $250,000 per year, plus an additional $150,000 per year for fringe benefits and operating expenses for two years. At the end of a two-year period, the dermatologist has utilized the entire $800,000 and generated $675,000 in net revenue. The best-case scenario is that the loan will be forgiven over time; nevertheless, depending on the year-two shortfall, the dermatologist is faced with the sobering reality of cutting expenses, such as personal salary, personnel, and benefits.

The advantage of the income guarantee model is that you have the freedom of being self-employed within a private practice; however, before accepting an income guarantee, you need to produce a business plan that outlines the volume projections by payer mix and is supported by a thorough market assessment. Note: Any entity willing to provide you with start-up costs should be amenable to producing a business plan for your practice.

Productivity Model

Productivity models take the form of classic capitation, where the physician is paid a lump sum to care for the patient for a given time period, or an adaptation, where a physician is paid a pre-set blended fee per patient seen, regardless of the services performed in the clinic. Additionally, there are numerous similar models that utilize the Work Relative Value Unit (WRVU). A WRVU is one of three components of a Relative Value Unit (RVU). A WRVU is a weighted numerical indicator that reflects complexity and time associated with the services provided. A more complex and time consuming service will be reflected in a higher WRVU and, consequently, a higher payment.

The WRVU is benchmarked nationally and by specialty by the Medical Group Management Association (MGMA). Much like the adapted capitation model, a physician may be paid a predefined amount per WRVU generated. It is common that the WRVU is benchmarked to determine how productive a physician is and, consequently, is utilized by an employer to determine a bonus amount or the following year's salary (if in an employed model). To learn more about WRVUs and productivity benchmarks, visit the MGMA website at mgma.com.

The advantage of the productivity model is that it provides a predetermined reimbursement amount per patient, which is blended or blind to the institution's payer mix, and it rewards you for the number of patients seen. Nevertheless, much like the income guarantee, thorough business planning is required to ensure that you will be able to generate your desired income while maintaining your quality of life. A number of physicians find themselves in the unenviable position of trading quality of life for quantity of income in a productivity model.

To reiterate, do the math before accepting the offer by dividing the projected overhead (your salary and benefits, staff salary and benefits, space, utilities, equipment, and supplies) by the per patient or WRVU reimbursement. This will provide you with an estimate of the number of patients you will have to see annually to generate your desired income.

How do you know that the salary or income potential you've been offered is competitive? To ensure that you can negotiate a deal that is fair and equitable, you need to answer this fundamental question. Fortunately, the following resources are available to help you determine if you have been offered compensation that is competitive within the healthcare market place:

- American Association of Medical Colleges (AAMC): Provides salary data for faculty physicians.

- American Medical Group Association (AMGA): Provides salary information by geographic region.

- Medical Group Management Association: Provides aggregate salary information by percentile.

Table 7 was abstracted with permission directly from Merritt Hawkins 2010 Review of Physician Recruiting Incentives (2010) and is an excellent example of the salaries being offered by specialty. Table 8, reprinted with permission from AMGA, highlights the median compensation by geographic region. Note: You should always utilize benchmark data to determine if your offer is fair and equitable within the competitive healthcare marketplace; a failure to do so is analogous to flying without instrumentation.

Table 7

Income Offered to Recruited Specialties, 2010

Specialty	Low	Average	High
Anesthesiology	$250,000	$331,000	$475,000
Cardiology (Invasive)	$325,000	$495,000	$680,000
Cardiology (Non-Invasive)	$315,000	$420,000	$600,000
Dermatology	$244,000	$314,000	$400,000
Emergency Medicine	$185,000	$247,000	$380,000
Endocrinology	$200,000	$219,000	$270,000
Family Practice	$140,000	$175,000	$255,000
Family Practice with Obstetrics	$155,000	$200,000	$320,000
Gastroenterology	$300,000	$411,000	$600,000
General Surgery	$175,000	$314,000	$410,000
Hospitalist	$165,000	$208,000	$295,000
Internal Medicine	$145,000	$191,000	$250,000
Medical Oncology	$300,000	$385,000	$500,000
Neurology	$180,000	$281,000	$460,000
OB/GYN	$175,000	$272,000	$350,000
Orthopedic Surgery	$300,000	$519,000	$825,000
Otolaryngology	$230,000	$349,000	$450,000
Pediatrics	$145,000	$180,000	$265,000
Psychiatry	$150,000	$200,000	$320,000
Pulmonology	$200,000	$305,000	$430,000
Radiology	$225,000	$417,000	$650,000
Urology	$250,000	$400,000	$550,000

Note. Base salary or income guarantee only, does not include production bonus or benefits.

Reprinted from the Merritt Hawkins an AMN Healthcare Company (www.merritthawkins.com). Reprinted with permission.

Table 8
AMGA 2010 Medical Group Compensation and Financial Survey

Specialty	Median Salary	Geographic Region			
		East	West	South	North
Allergy & Immunology	$241,138	$230,012	$264,040	$237,987	$225,836
Anesthesiology	$366,640	$326,667	$355,224	$352,625	$375,813
Cardiac & Thoracic Surgery	$507,143	$480,676	$570,076	$533,123	$539,209
Cardiology	$398,034	$349,369	$380,684	$424,379	$405,704
Colon & Rectal Surgery	$366,895	$364,000	$389,268	****	$350,531
Critical Care Medicine	$268,250	$257,728	$344,292	****	$264,750
Dermatology	$350,627	$325,543	$374,737	$319,157	$328,900
Diagnostic Radiology - Interventional	$478,000	$407,184	$464,542	$511,485	$478,000
Diagnostic Radiology - Non-Interventional	$438,115	$400,000	$445,000	$402,002	$445,169
Emergency Care	$267,293	$250,000	$300,383	$251,257	$279,531
Endocrinology	$212,281	$202,820	$207,718	$226,054	$223,790
Family Medicine	$197,655	$179,530	$208,996	$195,941	$192,475
Family Medicine - with Obstetrics	$202,047	****	****	****	$181,605
Gastroenterology	$389,385	$401,615	$385,611	$385,542	$394,417
General Surgery	$340,000	$316,380	$342,493	$316,184	$354,444
Geriatrics	$211,425	$189,910	$235,109	$170,970	$190,769
Gynecological Oncology	$406,000	$422,150	$374,384	****	$413,500
Gynecology	$218,607	$197,888	$204,951	$214,469	$241,750
Gynecology & Obstetrics	$294,190	$256,533	$307,055	$295,245	$297,775
Hematology & Medical Oncology	$315,133	$286,008	$331,372	$343,241	$315,719
Hospitalist	$211,835	$192,931	$213,798	$229,933	$210,217
Hypertension & Nephrology	$246,049	$235,000	$284,940	$256,293	$238,750
Infectious Disease	$222,094	$198,710	$247,056	$229,747	$227,750
Intensivist	$273,520	****	$265,419	****	****
Internal Medicine	$205,441	$202,862	$214,526	$203,375	$201,853
Neonatology	$265,000	$229,692	$336,280	$247,000	$282,356
Neurological Surgery	$548,186	$520,027	$560,422	$476,518	$562,047
Neurology	$236,500	$217,146	$248,040	$235,549	$236,500
Nuclear Medicine (M.D. only)	$414,500	****	$273,032	****	$364,393
Obstetrics	$301,773	****	****	$363,325	$290,299
Occupational / Environmental Medicine	$214,146	****	$212,126	****	$223,750
Ophthalmology	$325,384	$285,866	$321,726	$310,368	$354,500
Oral Surgery	$380,500	****	****	****	$414,750
Orthopedic Surgery	$476,083	$434,006	$494,863	$364,964	$482,193
Orthopedic-Medical	$265,345	****	$370,559	****	$190,850
Orthopedic Surgery - Joint Replacement	$580,711	****	$648,106	****	$554,343
Orthopedic Surgery - Hand	$465,006	****	$692,374	$460,148	$465,000
Orthopedic Surgery - Pediatrics	$424,367	****	****	$500,541	$408,296
Orthopedic Surgery - Spine	$641,728	****	$661,978	****	$608,286
Otolaryngology	$365,171	$335,000	$405,370	$338,019	$370,000
Pathology (M.D. only)	$344,195	$277,944	$335,648	$274,767	$354,750
Pediatric Allergy	$195,973	****	****	****	****
Pediatric Cardiology	$244,944	$225,691	$311,530	$236,680	$277,421
Pediatric Endocrinology	$185,901	$178,498	****	****	$187,200
Pediatric Gastroenterology	$236,700	$260,000	$311,193	****	$212,083
Pediatric Hematology / Oncology	$205,999	$167,813	$204,440	$209,997	$223,043
Pediatric Intensive Care	$265,913	$233,415	****	$259,206	$255,307

		Geographic Region			
Specialty	Median Salary	East	West	South	North
Pediatric Nephrology	$217,767	****	****	****	$218,630
Pediatric Neurology	$209,955	$195,085	****	****	$223,664
Pediatric Pulmonary Disease	$176,974	$172,794	****	$174,500	$201,750
Pediatric Surgery	$400,591	$350,352	****	$314,995	$432,354
Pediatrics & Adolescent	$202,832	$199,094	$212,740	$212,812	$195,951
Pediatric Infectious Disease	$199,165	****	****	****	$189,546
Perinatology	$394,121	$387,414	$359,726	$374,546	$423,054
Physical Medicine & Rehabilitation	$236,500	$222,459	$246,066	$240,090	$236,500
Plastic & Reconstruction	$388,929	$337,274	$398,393	$389,314	$414,185
Psychiatry	$208,462	$188,682	$246,547	$193,494	$198,500
Psychiatry - Child	$214,304	$199,169	$261,387	****	$205,875
Pulmonary Disease	$278,000	$249,311	$285,975	$271,529	$294,101
Radiation Therapy (M.D. only)	$413,518	$357,565	$452,837	$432,997	$415,250
Reproductive Endocrinology	$317,943	$327,329	$310,833	****	$339,250
Rheumatologic Disease	$219,411	$207,773	$222,165	$214,936	$220,952
Sports Medicine	$214,249	****	****	$223,130	$218,818
Transplant Surgery - Kidney	$348,000	****	****	****	$373,628
Transplant Surgery - Liver	$433,333	****	****	****	****
Trauma Surgery	$465,773	$392,695	****	$366,721	$406,318
Urgent Care	$215,625	$204,492	$215,184	$219,807	$218,251
Urology	$389,198	$391,590	$387,057	$425,066	$387,474
Vascular Surgery	$403,041	$392,946	$437,119	$384,006	$380,907

Note. Reprinted from the AMGA 2010 Medical Group Compensation and Financial Survey. ©2010, American Medical Group Association (www.amga.org). Reprinted with permission.

Case Study 1
Recruitment scenario

Outpatient internal medicine position (full-time) in the Midwest, "ability to make up to $300,000 annually."

- Employment Model: Employed by a regional healthcare firm
- Compensation Model: Net Revenue Model
- Market Potential: Excellent
- Call Coverage: None

The ability to make $300,000 per year without the burden of call coverage for an internist who had recently graduated from residency would seem too good to be true and, unfortunately, it was.

Reality

The reasonable and customary operating expenses deducted by the internist's employer were neither reasonable nor customary. Expenses included the following:

- Space and utilities.
- Staff and fringe benefits.
- Malpractice insurance.
- Equipment (depreciation expense).
- Supplies.
- Incidental and miscellaneous charges.
- Billing fee.
- 8% of gross charges (versus 8% of gross collections).

Being charged 8% by a billing company is not unreasonable if the billing company is assessing the 8% against the gross collections (reimbursement that the company collects on behalf of the physician). However, 8% of gross charges, independent of how successful the billing company is at reconciling and collecting on the claims filed, is unreasonable and had a significant affect on the internist's ability to generate a sufficient income in the net revenue compensation model. See Table 9.

The difference between the gross charges and gross collections cost the internist $78,000 in annual income. To compound the issue, the internist initially accepted a modest income guarantee while he established his practice, and by the time I interviewed him, he was in debt to his employer, working long hours, and generating an income that was not reflective of the number of hours he was working. The internist relayed to me that during any given pay period, one of his staff members might have a larger paycheck than his, all because of a single word within his contract ("charges" versus "collections").

Recommendations

- Understand the compensation model with which you will be working.
- Mitigate the known pitfalls through business planning and granular contractual language, which reduces and transfers, as much as possible, the financial risk from you to your employer.

Table 9
Do the Math

	8% of Gross Charges	8% of Gross Collections
Average charge per patient	$200	
Blended reimbursement per patient		$50
Number of patients per week	125	125
Revenue	$25,000	$6,250
x 8% billing fee	$2,000	$500
Weekly net reimbursement	$6,250	$6,250
Less 8%	$2,000	$500
	$4,250	$5,750
Annualized billing fees	$104,000	$26,000

Chapter 7
Patient Volume and the Pro Forma

Healthcare is a service industry, and you simply cannot have a successful or sustainable practice without patient volume. Although this statement may appear to be common knowledge, quantitatively assessing the market demand and determining a subsequent need for a physician isn't always practiced. A "build it and they will come" business mentality is not cavalier if the employer has contractual covenants shifting the financial burden to develop the patient volume onto the physician. The compensation model may mitigate the employer's financial risk, or the ability to terminate the physician without cause with a 90-day notice (see Chapter 11) ensures that the employer can quickly eliminate any financial burden incurred. With this stated, this chapter provides you with the basic tools necessary for determining if there is enough volume to support your practice and maintain your desired income. Always remember that the burden to demonstrate the market demand for your services belongs to the employer and the employer alone.

I was recently asked by a graduating resident physician to read and analyze an employment contract extended to him from a rural west coast hospital. During my review, I was immediately struck by the following five contractual terms:

- The salary was well above the national median.
- The physician had to provide 40 hours of patient contact per week (call coverage did not count).
- A failure to provide the required hours of patient contact would result in a salary adjustment for the physician.
- The hospital could terminate the contract with 90 days notice.

- The hospital could close the practice with 90 days notice.

The hospital was located in a town of 10,000 people, there were two physicians providing care within the same specialty, and a third physician was being recruited into a new position. I contacted the physician and asked him to e-mail the leadership of the hospital the following question: "How have you determined the need for a third physician?" The response was disappointingly predictable: "Dr. X is booking out for two months." This tells us nothing about the market demand for a third physician because we do not know how many patients are booking out, the number of days Dr. X is actually in clinic, how many patients Dr. X is willing to see on a clinic day, and so forth. Nevertheless, physicians are hired based on anecdotal information on a daily basis, and as highlighted by the previous example, held accountable for a lack of proper business planning.

Pro forma

To ensure there is enough patient volume to support your practice, your potential employer should provide you with a pro forma income statement. A pro forma "indicates hypothetical financial figures based on previous business operations for estimate purposes" (Pro Forma, 2010). Essentially, it will demonstrate the amount of volume (net patient services revenue) necessary to offset your expense exposure and ensure that your practice is self-sustaining. The following pro forma (Table 10) was developed to show how relatively minor fluctuations in WRVU productivity (patient volume) can transform a profitable practice into a losing venture. Additionally, it is designed to allow you (based on your compensation model) to have an armamentarium of tools (business vocabulary and fiscal comprehension) required to negotiate a practice arrangement that minimizes your personal financial vulnerability.

Table 10
Physician Practice Pro Forma

	Physician Practice Pro Forma			
		2011	2012	2013
1	**Revenue**			
2	Worked Relative Value Unites (WRVU)	8000	7500	7000
3	Reimbursement Per WRVU	$75	$75	$75
4	Gross Patient Services Revenue (GPSR)	$600,000	$562,500	$525,000
5	Less Uncompensated Care	($48,000)	($45,000)	($42,000)
6	***Net Patient Services Revenue (NPSR)***	*$552,000*	*$517,500*	*$483,000*
7	**Practice - Operating Expenses**			
8	Physician Salary	$200,000	$200,000	$200,000
9	Fringe Benefits Factor	$60,000	$60,000	$60,000
10	Staff Salaries	$70,000	$70,000	$70,000
11	Fringe Benefits Factor	$21,000	$21,000	$21,000
12	Payroll Taxes	$20,655	$20,655	$20,655
13	Liability Insurance	$10,000	$10,000	$10,000
14	Malpractice Insurance	$35,000	$35,000	$35,000
15	Rent	$18,000	$18,000	$18,000
16	Utilities	$2,400	$2,400	$2,400
17	Office Supplies	$1,500	$1,500	$1,500
18	Travel	$1,000	$1,000	$1,000
19	Postage	$500	$500	$500
20	Depreciation & Amortization	$0	$0	$0
21	Equipment Maintenance and Leasing	$24,000	$24,000	$24,000
22	Billing Fees	$26,000	$26,000	$26,000
23	**Total Practice Expenses**	$490,055	$490,055	$490,055
24	**Hospital - Administrative and General Expenses**			
25	Management Fees	$12,000	$12,000	$12,000
26	Technical Support Fees	$6,000	$6,000	$6,000
27	Other Fees	$0	$0	$0
28	**Total Hospital Expenses**	$18,000	$18,000	$18,000
29	***Total Operating Expenses***	*$508,055*	*$508,055*	*$508,055*
30	Earnings Before Taxes	$43,945	$9,445	($25,055)
31	Taxes	$6,592	$1,417	$0
32	***Net Income (Loss)***	*$37,353*	*$8,028*	*($25,055)*

The green highlight to the left of a pro forma line item indicates a specific area where I've seen physicians incur an unwelcome surprise once they commenced their respective practices. Each unanticipated reduction in revenue or unwelcome expense invariably placed the physicians in reactive positions where they had to scramble to produce additional revenue, if possible, or cut expenses.

Item #2: WRVUs & Item #3: Reimbursement per WRVU

Generally, the two scenarios in which you will be recruited are:

- As a replacement for an existing provider.
- Into a new position to create additional capacity.

Replacement

When recruited as a replacement, you need to request your predecessor's WRVU productivity for the 12 months prior to departure, as well as the average reimbursement per WRVU (all payers average). Once you have the data, you can place the information into your pro forma and extrapolate and forecast if your practice will be financially sustainable.

New position

A new position has the potential to be more financially hazardous than a replacement position, and it is imperative that you receive a copy of your potential employer's market assessment. To ensure that you can realistically forecast the level of productivity required to offset your salary, benefits, overhead, and other practice expenses, you can reverse engineer these expenses to determine the amount of WRVUs you will need to produce. Divide the Total Operating Expenses ($508,055) by the Average Reimbursement Per WRVU ($75) = 6774, multiply by 8% to cover the uncompensated care = 542, add the two numbers together, and you have a forecasted WRVU target of 7316 to break even. Once you've established the rough WRVU target, your employer needs to prove to you that the target is obtainable. Note: Some institutions will not separate the average reimbursement per WRVU and uncompensated care; meaning, the average reimbursement per WRVU will simply be less, or diluted. If you cannot obtain the average reimbursement per WRVU from your employer within your specialty, simply ask for a blended WRVU reimbursement for surgery or primary care, as applicable. If you are unable to obtain WRVU average reimbursement information, you should acquire a copy of the MGMA's annual Physician Compensation and Production Survey publication. You can use this reference book to crosswalk your salary (by percentile) to the WRVU productivity by the same percentile; thus, providing a rough estimate of your WRVU targets.

Always remember that the burden to demonstrate sufficient demand for your services belongs to your potential employer. One word of caution: Do not accept a market assessment showing the outward migration of patient referrals to other physicians as evidence that there is enough volume to support your practice. Although the volume may very well exist, how do you know that you will be able to redirect the referral streams? Again, the "build it and they will come" mentality does not eliminate professional relationships and the professional trust that has been established over time. The best way to mitigate the question of volume is to have your potential employer assume all the financial risk via the employed compensation model. As an employee, you can work diligently without assuming debt (income guarantee) or limiting your compensation (productivity and net revenue).

Item #5: Uncompensated Care

Some financial forecasts may separate the two primary components of uncompensated care by showing charitable care as a deduction from gross patient services revenue (GPSR) and bad debt as an operating expense; nevertheless, when creating a pro forma, it is important to have a sound estimate of the uncompensated care you will be providing. The first two years of your new position are vitally important as you work diligently to develop the patient volume necessary to maintain your practice. Additionally, you will be tasked to manage the delicate ecology between balancing your professional and personal lives, and the example pro forma demonstrates that if 8% of your GPSR becomes uncompensated care, it could determine the difference between breaking even or suffering a loss; thus, affecting your ability to maintain your desired staffing.

Items #9 & #11: Fringe Benefits Factors

Fringe benefits consist of paid time off (vacation, sick, and holiday), retirement contributions, health insurance, dental insurance, vision insurance, disability insurance, and more. The rule of thumb if this number cannot be determined beforehand is to multiply your salary and the salaries of each employee by 30% to create a fringe benefits estimate.

Item #12: Payroll Taxes & Item #31: Taxes

If you are going into a private practice or starting your practice with an income guarantee, you need to secure a certified public accountant (CPA) to provide the information you will need for payroll tax and income tax purposes. I've literally had physicians in my office, on the verge of bankruptcies, asking for personal loans to offset sizable unforeseen tax burdens.

Item #14: Malpractice Insurance

Please see Chapter 8.

Item #28: Total Hospital (or other) Expenses

I vividly remember having three separate discussions with three different physicians asking why their practices lost money when they were employed by the hospital and why they were making money, with the same direct expense exposure, now that they were self-employed in private practices. The answer, simply, is the indirect expense allocation from the hospital to their practices. The indirect expense exposure was allocated under an Administrative and General line item and accounted for a portion of my CEO salary and benefits, the chief financial officer's (CFO) salary and benefits, the chief of practice operations' salary and benefits, and so forth. In an academic setting, the indirect expenses may be represented as a dean's tax; nevertheless, the affect is interchangeable; meaning, it is an expense that decreases your net revenue. You must ensure that you fully comprehend and forecast all deductions from revenue when creating your pro forma.

Case Study 2
Recruitment scenario

General surgeon position (full-time) in the Northwest, $250,000 per year for two years (plus operating expenses).

- Employment Model: Private practice, hospital affiliated
- Compensation Model: Income guarantee from the local hospital
- Market Potential: Not defined
- Call Coverage: 1 in 4

The salary wasn't competitive with the national median; nevertheless, the location was desirable for the young surgeon and his family, and he was "sold" on the potential to generate an income that would exceed the guarantee.

Reality

The market demand for a fourth surgeon was not defined, and there was a competing group of surgeons in an adjacent town controlling the secondary market. For two years, the general surgeon worked tirelessly to redirect referral streams and generate the patient volume necessary to sustain his practice. Two and a half years after he started, I interviewed the general surgeon and was saddened during our dinner conversation to hear that he had depleted his family savings, his wife was going to place the children in daycare and find a job, he was putting his house on the market, he had a six-figure debt to the hospital that was accruing interest, and it appeared his only option was to file for bankruptcy. As I sat across the table listening to the general surgeon provide me with detail after detail of how he tried to produce volume, his wife sat silently and began to cry. He honestly believed he was recruited to provide a better call rotation (1 in 4 versus 1 in 3), and he was now being held accountable for the hospital's lack of due diligence and his good faith.

Recommendations

- First and foremost, the burden to demonstrate that there is enough volume to support your practice belongs to your potential employer, so be sure to request copies of the market assessment.

- Work with your potential employer to develop a pro forma to ensure that you comprehend your volume projections and expense exposure (use a CPA if you are going into a private practice).

- Make sure all volume projections are supported by a market analysis, and if there are competing physicians, speak to members of the medical staff to determine if you can redirect the patient migration.

- If you are not completely confident the volume exists, shift the financial burden to the employer by requesting an employed compensation model (you should never be held responsible for an employer's lack of business planning).

Chapter 8
Malpractice Insurance

After presenting a talk on common contractual pitfalls to a group of resident physicians, I overheard one resident make the following telling statement to a colleague: "I didn't know there were different types of malpractice insurance."

If residents are graduating from training programs not aware that there are different types of malpractice insurance, they are simply not in positions to comprehend the personal financial liability they could incur if their contracts are not structured appropriately.

There are two major genres of malpractice insurance:

- Claims Made: Covers claims filed within the dates for which you are covered by the insurance.

- Per Occurrence: Covers claims for dates of service that occurred when the policy was in effect.

Although the basic premises of the insurances are similar (covering malpractice claims), the major nuance is the length of the coverage.

Claims Made

A claims-made policy will cover you while you have the insurance; however, once the policy is no longer in effect, you are not covered. For example, if you have a claims-made policy from January 1, 2010 to December 31, 2012, and a malpractice suit is filed against you on June 15, 2012 for a service provided on February 8, 2010, you are covered. However, if the malpractice suit is filed against you on January 1, 2015 for the same date of service (February 8, 2010), you are "bare" (meaning you have no coverage). Even though the "act" occurred when you had insurance coverage, it is dependent upon when the act occurred and when the claim is filed.

Per Occurrence

A per-occurrence policy will cover dates of service when the policy was in effect even if the policy is no longer active. For example, if you have a per-occurrence policy from January 1, 2010 to December 31, 2012, and a malpractice suit is filed against you on June 15, 2012 for a service provided on February 8, 2010, you are covered. Additionally, if the malpractice suit is filed against you on January 1, 2015 for the same date of service (February 8, 2010), you are covered, because the "act" occurred during your coverage period.

From an employer's perspective, the major difference between the two types of insurance is cost. A claims-made policy will become more expensive as it "matures." So, during the first year, it will cost less because there is less risk exposure, and during the second year, it will become more expensive because of the increased risk accrual. Nevertheless, the claims-made policy will be less expensive initially and over the term of your employment (in aggregate) for your employer. The common contractual pitfall for graduating resident physicians and early careerists is not knowing the type of malpractice under which they are covered, and if it is a claims-made policy, not negotiating who will pay for the cost of the "tail" insurance.

As previously stated, a claims-made policy covers negligent acts/malpractice while the policy is in effect, and to ensure that you are not personally financially vulnerable for a suit that is filed after the claims-made policy is terminated, you need to be provided with tail insurance to cover previous acts during a defined period of time. Tail insurance is expensive, generally costing between 150% to 200% of a mature claims-made policy. The cost of the claims-made policy will differ depending upon specialty and geography; nevertheless, to illustrate the potential financial burden, consider the following:

A mature OB/GYN claims-made policy in a rural relatively non-litigious state could cost $35,000 per year. If the OB/GYN physician decided to move, and the tail coverage wasn't provided in the contract, the physician would need to come up with $70,000 to ensure that "prior acts" were covered or negotiate "nose" coverage with the new employer. Nose coverage can be purchased by you or your employer and will be added to your new policy to cover prior acts.

Finally, you need to ensure you understand the terms of your malpractice policy. For example, does your malpractice policy cover your out-of-pocket legal fees or only the settlement or suit award? We live in a litigious society, and there are generally never any positive financial surprises. Remember, per-occurrence costs more; however, you do not require tail or nose coverage. Claims made will leave you bare if you do not acquire tail or nose coverage. To mitigate your personal financial risk, please see the recommendations and proposed contractual language at the end of this chapter.

Case Study 3
Recruitment scenario

Family practice position (full-time) in the Southeast, $120,000 under an evergreen contract.

- Employment Model: Hospital employed
- Compensation Model: Employed model
- Market Potential: Excellent
- Call Coverage: 1 in 6

This was actually a family practice couple looking to relocate to be closer to family.

Reality

The couple was engaging, and during the interview process, I went through my list of common contractual pitfalls to determine the potential for an unwelcome financial surprise if they decided to join my medical staff. The couple had an attorney friend who had reviewed their contracts, and he did an excellent job, as evidenced by a preponderance of my pitfall questions being covered contractually. Nevertheless, there was one pitfall not defined within their contractual covenants. Their contracts stated that the hospital would provide malpractice insurance with limits at the industry standard; however, they did not list the type of malpractice insurance. When I asked what type of malpractice coverage was provided by the hospital, the husband stated he would call his employer and let me know at dinner. Later that evening, I learned it was a claims-made policy, and that the tail responsibility fell to the physicians. The physicians were surprised—they were under the impression the costs associated with malpractice insurance would be covered by the employer (remember, if a covenant isn't written down, it doesn't exist). Unfortunately, they were wrong. With the cost of the tail and/or the nose coverage into the six-figure range, they didn't have the money required to ensure coverage for prior acts, and I simply could not extend the capital required to free them from their current positions. Faced with this sobering reality, they decided to return to their Southeast hospital and stop looking for new employment opportunities.

Recommendations

- You need to know what type of malpractice insurance your employer will be providing for you, as well as what it covers.

- If it is a claims-made policy, make sure you negotiate that your employer is required to pay for the tail insurance. One way to soften this negotiating stance is to base the tail coverage on tenure, as highlighted in the following contractual language:

If the Physician is employed for less than one (1) year, he/she will pay for 100% of the tail insurance. If the Physician is employed for more than one (1) year and less than two (2) years, the Physician and the Employer will share in the cost of the tail insurance, with each party paying 50%. If the Physician is employed for two (2) years or longer, the Employer will be responsible for 100% of the cost of the tail insurance. The tail insurance will be at the same coverage limits as when the contract was in effect.

Chapter 9
Call Expectations

Most hospitals take a hands-off approach to call by having physicians within specific specialty disciplines coordinate their own call schedules. This work-it-out-amongst-yourselves approach, coupled with the common contractual language stipulating that physicians are responsible for taking an equitable share of call, could potentially create a perfect storm, where an "equitable share" becomes an unsustainable burden. Consider the following:

If you are recruited into a scenario where your call coverage is 1 in 7 (1 day of call every 7th day), and your contract stipulates an equitable share, you will enjoy your promised call rotation as long as there is no physician turnover within your call group. However, when turnover occurs (and it will), your equitable share will increase proportionately to the number of physicians remaining, and you will have no contractual basis to reduce this obligation.

When I became a CEO, I inherited two specialists who had taken a 1-in-2-call rotation for well over a decade, and because they were in a private practice, they were never compensated for this burden. Although call can be utilized to help build a practice, due to the hospital's poor payer mix (quantity of Medicaid and uncompensated care patients), the specialists were not able to offset their every-other-day time commitment with comparable compensation. The specialists approached me, not willing to take more than a 1-in-3 rotation during the week and only one weekend per month. Pursuant to my institution's medical staff bylaws (see Chapter 5), I could have forced the specialists to continue to take 1-in-2 call; nevertheless, I tried to be diplomatic and offered the specialists a cash stipend for call above and beyond their requested rotation (this allows for continuous coverage and saves the hospital thousands of dollars on locum tenens expenses). Much to my surprise and chagrin, the specialists turned down the additional compensation. The situation left me angered and perplexed until I was approached by a seasoned member of the medical staff who helped me comprehend the issue by informing me that for many physicians, time is more valuable than money. The conversation culminated with him making the following poignant declaration: "I will not lose my second wife and second set of children because I'm simply not there for them." Coming from a respected physician, who had taken continuous practice call for his patients in a 1-in-3 emergency department rotation for over a decade, the point was well made and easily understood.

When joining a practice, a medical group, a department, or a hospital, it is important that you understand your call burden and the types of call coverage you will be providing. Although this may appear to be rudimentary, I've reviewed physician employment contracts making no reference to call, and I've seen physicians immediately disappointed when their assumed 1-in-7 call was increased to a frequency of 1 in 4 because the partners were unwilling to participate in the call coverage (having paid their "dues").

The following list is an example of the different forms of call for which I've seen physicians provide coverage:

- Emergency department.
- Practice/outpatient.
- Inpatient.
- Telephone (to help buffer emergency department and practice call).
- Secondary (back-up call rotation).

Although the response expectations will differ depending on the type of call (physically responding to the emergency department versus returning a phone call), the burden of being tied to a pager or cell phone will limit your time off and affect your ability to balance your professional and personal lives contemporaneously.

In contracting, the wording of each covenant must be granular, non-ambiguous, and easily interpreted. Anything that is left to interpretation, as a rule of thumb, will not work to your advantage. As it applies to call coverage, each type of coverage needs to be defined within the contract, and the best way to eliminate an unsustainable call burden is to replace the "equitable share" language with "not to exceed." To ensure that you are perceived as a team player, you should always consider including vacation coverage; nevertheless, the following "not to exceed" language will protect your from taking a disproportionate share of call:

Physician will provide practice call and emergency department call concurrently that will not exceed a rotation greater than one (1) day of call every fifth (5th) day, with the exception of vacation coverage. Physician's call rotation may exceed one (1) day of call every fifth (5th) day to cover for vacations; nevertheless, the additional coverage shall not exceed two (2) consecutive weeks (14 days) or thirty (30) total days in any calendar year. Any or all other call rotations not defined within this contract are declared null and void.

Analysis: The contract language provided above assumes you were promised a call rotation of 1 in 5 and that you will be providing both practice and emergency department call. By creating language that stipulates you are taking both forms of call concurrently, this will ensure that you always have a 1-in-5 rotation (versus being on call for the practice and then following it with a night of emergency department call). The vacation coverage allows you to support your colleagues, as you would want to be supported; however, it protects you from taking a disproportionate share as a junior member of the staff and hedges against enhanced call coverage due to maternity leave and/or sabbaticals. Additionally, by including language about all other forms of call, you are protecting your time against the potential of future non-defined call rotations being created. Finally, if you are amenable to taking additional call as a mechanism to generate additional compensation, make sure this is detailed within your contract. I've written employment contracts that paid physicians a defined amount of money per day for additional call. This saved my institution money on locums tenens and allowed for continuous coverage for our services. Note: If you include this language, be sure that you have the right of refusal. Remember the lesson taught to me: Time is more valuable than money.

Case Study 4
Recruitment scenario

Anesthesiologist position (part-time) in the Midwest, $150,000 under an evergreen contract.

- Employment Model: Hospital employed
- Compensation Model: Employed model
- Market Potential: Excellent
- Call Coverage: 1 in 4

The anesthesiologist was a single, dedicated mother who wanted to ensure she could provide for her daughter without sacrificing their time together.

Reality

As word got out that I was willing to help physicians with their employment contracts, the aforementioned anesthesiologist contacted me through a mutual colleague, and she asked me to review her contract. During our first discussion, I asked her to relay to me the recruitment promises made to her during the interview process (see Chapter 3), and then I asked for a copy of her employment contract. I had several issues with the contract, the most critical being the call coverage expectations the single mother would be contractually obligated to provide. Although she was promised that her call burden would not exceed 1 in 4, the contract stated that she would take an equitable share of call, and the hospital only had one other anesthesiologist on staff. Contractually, she would have been obligated to provide 1-in-2 call (every other night, every other weekend, and every other holiday). After I relayed my concerns to her, the anesthesiologist met with the hospital's CEO and the vice president (VP) of human resources and during the negotiating process, she became so concerned with the dialogue that she asked if they could take a 10-minute break. During the "break," the anesthesiologist called me from the parking lot and told me the CEO was playing the trust card, stating that professional relationships are built on trust and that every nuance could not be captured contractually. The VP underscored the CEO's assertion by stating that she had good notes and that the "spirit" of the agreement would be fulfilled. I told the anesthesiologist that if it isn't written down, it doesn't exist and that even though I was certain the CEO and VP were people of integrity, if they left, the spirit of what was agreed upon left with them. I simply told her to stay strong, have the VP type up the notes, and use them as an addendum to the contract.

Recommendations

- Make sure that each type of call is spelled out within your contract and that the language states, "not to exceed" versus an equitable share.
- If you are expected to provide more than one type of call, add the concurrent language referenced in this chapter to minimize your aggregate call burden.

Chapter 10
Free Money = Time Commitment

I use the preceding picture as a slide for my contracting presentation to residents and early careerists to illustrate that money is used to accomplish the following two things:

- Lure you to a position.

- Hook you for a predetermined period of time.

The competition to recruit and retain physicians has become increasingly intense; consequently, employers who seek to have a competitive advantage in the marketplace are becoming creative with the financial incentives they are willing to provide in exchange for services. The following list highlights the most common financial incentives provided to physicians for accepting open positions:

- Tuition reimbursement.

- Sign-on bonus.

- Relocation expenses.

- Equity share of a mortgage.

- Pre-employment stipends.

- Other loans/monetary commitments.

The following section of this chapter is dedicated to analyzing each incentive and providing contractual language or clarification to ensure that each concession works to your advantage, without hindering your ability to change jobs.

Tuition reimbursement

Physicians are leaving residency with substantial undergraduate and medical school debt, and potential employers are willing to help early careerists pay off their loans to ensure tenure. Generally, I believe this incentive is mutually beneficial for the employer and physician; however, it must be structured appropriately and reflected within your contract. Although it may be very tempting to take a lump sum payment of, for this example, $100,000, you need to know that it will be counted as income and that income taxes will be deducted. Additionally, the payment will lock you contractually to your employer for a "forgiveness" period of time as demonstrated by the following sample contract language:

The tuition reimbursement will be forgiven over a period of five (5) years ($20,000 per year). If, for any reason, you are no longer employed by Name of Employer and/or are no longer providing full-time healthcare services, forty (40) hours of patient contact time per week, to the Name of Employer's community within a timeframe of five (5) years, you will be expected to repay a prorated amount of the tuition reimbursement back to Name of Employer with interest, prime plus 1% as established by the Wall Street Journal.

To eliminate the time commitment, do not take any upfront money; on the contrary, request that for every 12 months of service worked that you are provided $20,0000 in tuition reimbursement (up to $100,000). You will still receive the full benefit of the tuition reimbursement without incurring a debt that is forgiven over time. Additionally, your contract language should specify that, if you leave within any given year, a prorated amount of the $20,000 will be provided to you based on the number of months worked prior to your departure.

Sign-on bonus

The sign-on bonus has become increasingly more common, and like tuition reimbursement, it is generally forgiven over time. With this stated, if you structure the sign-on bonus with language that is analogous to the aforementioned tuition reimbursement example, you are essentially transforming your sign-on bonus into a retention bonus. If you need the upfront money, the key is to minimize the length of the forgiveness period. I recommend never exceeding two years for the forgiveness of a sign-on bonus. Remember, if you leave, for any reason, within two years, you will have to pay a prorated share of your sign-on bonus back with interest.

Relocation expenses

It is reasonable and customary for your employer to provide you with a relocation allowance not to exceed $10,000. What is not reasonable is to have a forgiveness period for moving expenses. Still, I've seen increasingly more contracts list a forgiveness period for this traditional recruitment expense. Read your contract carefully and, if applicable, delete the forgiveness period for relocation/moving expenses.

Equity share of a mortgage

Before the collapse of the housing market, this was a popular recruitment tool to ensure that a physician had "roots" in an employer's service area. Essentially, the employer would provide up to 20% of the purchase cost of a house and "own" an equitable percentage of the value; thus, allowing a physician to purchase a house that may not have been in the physician's price range initially. The downside to the equity share of a mortgage is that for your employer, it is an investment; meaning, if you invest your time and money into your house, your employer's 20% will appreciate in value. Specifically, when you sell, you will not be repaying the 20% initially invested. On the contrary, you will be handing over 20% of the purchase price. Note: The employer does assume financial risk if your house sells for less than the original purchase price. The key contractual language if you plan on taking advantage of the equity share of a mortgage is that you, and you alone, retain the decision-making authority of when to sell the house.

Pre-employment stipends

There are a number of employers who are willing to offer stipends to residents in difficult-to-recruit specialties during the last year or two of their residencies. It goes without saying that residents work long hours for nominal pay, and being offered additional compensation can be quite enticing.

I was recently approached by a resident who wanted my counsel after he was contacted by a hospital company and offered $2,500 per month for his last two years of residency, and in return, the physician would work for the company after graduation for a period of two years. My first question was, "Do you need the money?" After hearing that he did not, I told him I thought it was very clever that the company would be able to secure a specialist for two years on a $60,000 investment. I also highlighted that the employer did not have to employ him and that he would be handing away his options and his negotiating leverage by accepting the money. The resident decided not to take the stipend.

Other loans/monetary commitments

As previously stated, all monetary commitments are used to lure and hook you to a position for a period of time. Judiciously weigh your need for capital against the time commitment, and remember that the more monetary commitments you accept, the more encumbered your departure will become.

A word of caution: You need to know if any/all upfront money you accept will be expensed against your practice (see Chapter 7). Depending on your compensation model (income guarantee or net revenue, for example), you could be starting your practice with unanticipated and significant debt, which will limit/offset your practice expenses and your desired income.

Case Study 5
Recruitment scenario

Orthopedic surgeon position (full-time) in the Northeast, $500,000 per year under a three-year contract.

- Employment Model: Hospital employed
- Compensation Model: Employed model
- Market Potential: Excellent
- Call Coverage: 1 in 3
- Upfront Money:
    $10,000 for moving expenses.
    $40,000 sign-on bonus.
    $100,000 for tuition reimbursement.

The orthopedic surgeon was graduating residency with significant debt and was looking for help with his medical school loans.

Reality

All upfront money, including the relocation/moving expenses, were considered interest-accruing loans (prime plus 1%), which would be forgiven over time. To complicate matters, the $150,000 in total upfront money would be forgiven over a period of three years on different time schedules. Forgiveness for the relocation/moving expenses would begin on the first day of employment, as would forgiveness for the sign-on bonus. However, forgiveness for the $100,000 in tuition reimbursement would commence on the first day of the second year; meaning that the "loan" would not be completely forgiven until the orthopedic surgeon completed four years of service—on a three year contract!

Recommendations

- Minimize the amount of upfront money you take, and mitigate your time commitment by negotiating a forgiveness period that does not exceed two years.

- Understand that relocation/moving expenses are reasonable and customary and should not be considered a loan that is forgiven over time.

- Ensure that you know, prior to accepting any upfront compensation, if and how the financial benefits will be expensed against your practice.

Chapter 11
Termination Covenants

You enjoy your work, your kids are thriving in the local school system, and your spouse feels at home within the local community. At 7:30 a.m., you attend your monthly practice meeting with the organization's leadership to review the financial performance of your clinic. You've been working hard to build your patient volume for the last two years, and although the practice has made great financial strides, it still isn't breaking even due to an unfavorable payer mix. Nevertheless, your WRVU productivity demonstrates the sweat equity you've invested into the practice, and you feel confident that your effort will be rewarded.

The meeting begins with a review of your practice financials, and the discussion quickly transitions into the leader stating that the institution needs to make difficult decisions based on current financial performance. Before you can ask a question of clarification, the leader hands you a letter and informs you that you are being terminated without cause and that your last day, pursuant to your employment contract, is 90 days from today. In the midst of the disappointment and shock, the reality sets in—you will need to find a new job; sell your house; uproot your children and re-enroll them in new schools; and take your spouse out of a desirable community. How can this be accomplished in 90 days?

The fictitious scenario highlighted above could become a brutal reality if you don't protect yourself contractually. Employee contract termination language may be located in one or several of the following standard termination covenants:

- Termination for specific breaches.
- Termination due to closure.

- Termination by physician.

- Termination for violation of employment policies.

- Termination without cause.

- Effect of termination.

To ensure you understand and are able to mitigate the potential personal ramifications attached to each termination clause, each covenant is briefly analyzed below and, if applicable, sample language is provided to minimize the affect and mitigate the abruptness of being terminated.

Termination for specific breaches

A vast preponderance of, if not all, healthcare employment contracts will include this clause, which will essentially end your employment if:

- You cannot be credentialed or re-credentialed as a member of the medical staff (see Chapter 5).

- You cannot obtain or maintain your medical licensure.

- You lose or have restrictions against your Drug Enforcement Agency (DEA) registration.

- You have exclusions or sanctions from federal and state health insurance programs (Medicare or Medicaid).

- You have failed to provide the services outlined within the contract.

Generally, all contracts will give you an opportunity to "cure" the breach; nevertheless, if you are not generating revenue, be aware that you most likely will not be paid during this time (which will affect the extension of your fringe benefits). Although this covenant is customary and reasonable from an employer's perspective, I strongly recommend negotiating that you are paid during the "cure" period. Additionally, you need to understand your expectations (productivity, medical staff citizenship, comportment, and so forth) on a granular level and unequivocally concur that all are immediately achievable, or you will run the risk of being terminated for breach of contract.

Termination due to practice closure

If you are employed by a group practice, it is not unreasonable to have your employment terminated because your practice closes. However, if you are in a solo practice, it is unreasonable to have the practice closed and your employment terminated with 30 days notice. If you are a solo practitioner, I strongly encourage you to eliminate this language. If you are in a group or hospital-employed practice, I recommend increasing the length of notice to 180 days. A six-month notice is a reasonable amount of time to find another job, locate housing, and move your family (versus 30 days).

Termination by physician

This covenant allows you to hold your employer accountable for material breaches of the contract and provides for the same general 30-day opportunity to cure the breach. Additionally, some contracts use this covenant to include language about disabilities, medical conditions, retirement, or the sale of the employing entity. If the entity that employs you is sold, you want to ensure that your contract is still in effect and, depending upon your fit with your new employer, that you have an unobstructed opportunity to leave with 90 days notice.

Termination for violation of employment polices

You need a copy of the employee handbook and all applicable employee policies before beginning your employment. You also need to know your due process, not just under the medical staff bylaws/rules and regulations of the medical staff, but as an employee. For egregious breaches of policy, your termination could be swift, with no recourse; with this stated, you have a responsibility to understand and comprehend the code of conduct to which you will be accountable.

Termination without cause

Every hospital employment contract I've reviewed has contained a variation of the following clause:

Either party may terminate this employment contract at any time, and without cause, upon ninety (90) days written notice of the intent to terminate to the other party.

In my experience, if there are behavioral issues or issues of productivity, it will be discussed with the physician; however, instead of going through the institutional due process, which can be painful and disruptive, the fastest way to end the relationship is to terminate without cause. I generally counsel physicians to delete this covenant and replace it with a notice period clause outlining the length of notice you must provide before separation. If the employer is unwilling to remove the language, apply the 90/180 rule when negotiating. This rule calls for you to provide a minimum 90 days notice of your intent to leave, and your employer must provide you with 180 days notice of their intent to terminate the contract. A six-month notice will eliminate an abrupt end to your employment and will provide you and, if applicable, your family, with enough time to ensure smooth professional and personal transitions versus being caught short by a three-month notice. Note: Make sure you remove any language in the contract allowing your employer to terminate the agreement early if you provide notice. The premise behind restructuring this covenant is to provide you with enough time to transition, and to allow the employer to terminate you during your notice period would have an antithetical impact.

Effect of termination

This covenant highlights that the employer has no responsibility to pay you or extend benefits to you or your family past the date of termination (you can obtain COBRA coverage; however, it is expensive). The effect of termination language underscores the need to contractually protect you, and your family, from an abrupt or unexpected end to your employment.

Case Study 6
Recruitment scenario:

Urologist position (full-time) in the Midwest, $350,000 per year under an evergreen contract.

- Employment Model: Multi-specialty group employed
- Compensation Model: Employed model with net revenue bonus
- Market Potential: Good
- Call Coverage: 1 in 4

The urologist was returning to his rural hometown to be closer to his family after running a successful private practice in the Southeast for 20 years.

Reality

The urologist was happy to be back in his hometown and within weeks of returning, he and his family immediately began renovating their dream house. However, there was underlying tension within the multi-specialty group practice, with the urologist's personality clashing with the culture of his employer. The tension manifested in occasional heated discussions with staff members and, consequently, the urologist confronted the operating partners to let them know that he believed the behavior of the staff was disrespectful, and that he felt unsupported by some of his colleagues in the group that were defending the staff. The operating partners attempted to assuage the situation by meeting with the staff and the urologist, providing direct feedback and creating expectations for collaborative behavior. Nevertheless, the situation was not resolved, and it periodically resurfaced over the next two months. Five months after returning to his hometown, the urologist requested to meet with the managing partners to discuss the ongoing conflict and was horrified when the meeting ended with a 90-day termination-without-cause letter. The urologist ended up in a position in which he had to move because of the termination-without-cause and non-compete covenants in his contract (see Chapter 12), and he was facing personal financial ruin, having invested the money from the sale of his private practice into his dream house, which was far from complete. The disruption to his family was swift—his children were in school, and his siblings were devastated when they were told he would be leaving. In the end, the urologist returned to the Southeast and was desperately trying to sell his unfinished house (he stopped the renovations to mitigate his personal financial losses).

Recommendations

- Know, on a granular level, the covenants of your employment contract and ensure that any unreasonable expectations are modified to protect yourself against the potential to breach; additionally, ensure that you are still being paid and that your full benefits are still in effect during the "cure" period.

- Understand the employment policies and due process of your employer prior to commencing your practice by asking for a copy of the employee handbook and/or code of conduct policies.

- Make sure your employer cannot terminate the contract during your separation notice period.

- If possible, replace the termination-without-cause language with a notice period clause defining the length of notice you must provide your employer. If your potential employer refuses to eliminate the termination-without-cause covenant, mitigate the potential impact with the 90/180 rule.

Chapter 12
Non-Compete Covenants

Non-compete covenants generally have two defining factors—distance and time. However, they can take on many different forms, which are literally peppered throughout an employment contract. From loyalty clauses to language prohibiting the use of proprietary information, all non-compete covenants are designed for the same purpose: To ensure that you are unable to continue practicing in the same primary market as your employer.

I do not disagree with the basic premise behind a standard non-compete clause. There are considerable upfront costs your employer is investing in you and your practice, and if you decide to leave and hang out your shingle down the street, your employer has essentially financed its own competition. The following sample non-compete language is provided to emphasize the potential drawbacks of which you should be cognizant and to highlight the language that will need to be revised, added, and/or deleted to ensure that contract is equitable to both parties:

Non-Compete Covenant: *Acknowledging the Medical Group's financial investment being received by the Physician pursuant to this employment contract, so long as Physician continues employment by the Medical Group,* ***for a period of five (5) years****, the Physician shall not take any ownership,* ***either directly or indirectly, through ownership by Physician's spouse or immediate family members, in any entity or medical practice, or be employed to practice medicine by any practice or enterprise, that competes with the Medical Group within the Medical Group's primary service area which is defined as a 50-mile radius*** *of the Medical Group's practice locations, as traveled in the most direct route possible. Physician agrees that the Medical Group shall be entitled to enforce this covenant not to compete through legal relief in any court with jurisdiction in the Name of State. Given the significant monetary investment the Medical Group will put forth to commence* *and build the Physician's practice, it is unequivocally agreed to by the Physician that the above-described non-compete restrictions of geographic location and time have been given ample thought and reflection by the Physician and the Physician agrees that they are required to protect the Medical Group's initial financial investment and ongoing financial interests. Additionally, if the Medical Group is forced to seek legal relief as a result of a violation of this covenant by the Physician,* **Physician shall pay for all of Medical Group's legal fees associated with enforcing this covenant.**

Language to be revised

Any non-compete covenant that is longer than two years or has a geographic restriction greater than 25 miles is unreasonable and should be revised as such.

Language to be deleted

If your spouse is a medical professional (physician, nurse, or physical therapist, for example), this covenant needs to be deleted because it would prevent your spouse from working for a competing practice or institution, potentially even going into a private practice. Additionally, never sign any contractual covenant transferring the financial liability for "reasonable legal/attorney's fees." If you have a legitimate challenge to the non-compete covenant or any other contractual term and you lose the legal challenge, you will be saddled with your legal fees and those of the employer.

Language to be added

The sample non-compete covenant is missing a clause that would negate and void the non-compete covenant in its entirety if you were terminated without cause, the practice closed, or you and the medical group parted ways amicably (in good standing). The following sample language would allow you to open a practice in the medical group's primary service area based on the aforementioned termination scenarios:

Medical Group shall waive the provisions of the non-compete covenant if this employment contract is terminated by the Medical Group without cause; if the Medical Group is sold or merged with another entity or declares bankruptcy; if the Medical Group is unable to financially comply with financial obligations listed within this employment contract; or upon the mutual written agreement between the Physician and the Medical Group. If the provisions of the non-compete covenant are waived, the Medical Group shall also waive any covenant as it applies to the Physician's ability to contact his/her panel of patients and any proprietary information clause that would hinder and/or disrupt the Physician from providing continuous care to his/her patients.

Also, be aware of language that is prohibitive of external activity and/or vague or ambiguous. Language that is prohibitive of external activity could disallow you from providing locums coverage to generate additional income or working in a volunteer capacity. If this language is not within your contract, do not assume that you will be covered by your employing entity's malpractice coverage if you are working within this capacity. Generally, a vast majority of all healthcare employers will not extend malpractice coverage into environments they do not control through policies and protocols. If the language pertaining to outside activities is vague or ambiguous, your employer could easily interpret that any personal revenue generated by your activities belongs to the practice, and not you. If you think this is unlikely, I've seen this become a contentious topic that becomes heightened if the practice or employer is losing money and/or is financially constrained. To eliminate the potential conflict, and to purposefully be redundant, make sure your contractual language for this, and all covenants, is granular and easily interpreted.

Case Study 7
Recruitment scenario

Internal medicine outpatient-only position (full-time) in the Northeast, $150,000 per year for two years.

- Employment Model: Private practice
- Compensation Model: Income guarantee
- Market Potential: Not defined
- Call Coverage: 1 in 8

The internist wanted to stay in the rural Northeast and was provided start-up funding for her practice by a local hospital.

Reality

A primary care network consisting of internists and family practitioners had been entrenched within the rural and medical communities for 15 to 20 years and dominated the local market. The internist worked diligently to build her practice, and to prevent incurring a significant debt to the hospital, she used the income guarantee sparingly. After 12 months of practice, it was clear to the internist that she would not be able to generate enough volume to sustain her practice and generate a reasonable income. The internist understood that she would have to repay the used portion of the income guarantee back to the hospital (see Chapter 6); nevertheless, she was determined to remain in the rural Northeast. The internist scheduled a meeting with the leadership of the hospital to share her plans for relocating to another practice location within the state (outside of the hospital's primary market) and to establish a payment schedule to repay the portion of the income guarantee she had used throughout the year. The meeting did not go well, and the hospital leaders informed her she would not be allowed to practice at her desired location, 43 miles from her current practice site, due to the non-compete covenant in her contract. Unfortunately, the non-compete covenant the physician signed did not include the two defining factors of time and distance. Essentially, the physician signed a non-compete that would not allow her work at any location at any point of time. The physician was angry and bitter. Having worked for a year, generating an income that was significantly less than her peer group and incurring a debt to the hospital, she was not in a position to challenge the hospital legally on a non-compete covenant that could easily be interpreted as unreasonable and not enforceable. Nevertheless, she had no choice but to incur the additional debt and expend the emotional capital required to litigiously fight the non-compete covenant.

Recommendations

- If possible, eliminate any/all non-compete covenants. If not possible, ensure that the non-compete has the two defining factors (distance and time).
- Distance should not be greater than the primary service area of your employer or 25 miles (the lesser of the two).
- Time should not be greater than two years.
- Add language that eliminates the non-compete clause if you are terminated without cause; your employer is sold, merged, or files for bankruptcy; or your employer cannot comply with the obligations listed within your employment contract.

- Ensure that any language referring to proprietary information is eliminated as well.
- Ensure that any language that refers to external activities, non-compete or otherwise, is granular and easily interpreted.

Chapter 13
Miscellaneous Contractual Pitfalls

The preeminent contracting pitfalls are outlined in the preceding chapters; however, there are still nuances (minor pitfalls that could become major themes for job dissatisfaction) to underscore and to which you should pay attention. From partnerships to time off, the theme of this guide remains consistent; you need granular language to ensure your interpretation of the contractual covenants matches your employer's and that it will survive any/all leadership turnover.

Equipment

You may have been promised during the recruitment process that you would have the tools and equipment required to perform optimally within your specialty. Nevertheless, if you don't capture your equipment needs contractually (granularly, down to the preferred vendor), you create the risk of needing to use existing equipment and/or going without equipment, as the requests are subjected to your employer's budgeting process. If you are in a surgical specialty that is going to be employed by a private practice, make sure your employer provides you with a letter from the applicable hospital outlining the obligation to provide you with your preferred instrumentation. The same premise applies to office furnishings—if you are promised a renovated office and with new furniture, it should be reflected within your contract.

Partnerships

Physicians of all specialties are accepting compensation that is considerably less than the regional median, based on the premise that they will be rewarded with significant income increases when they become full partners in three to five years.

The problem with this scenario is that a majority of physicians don't understand that for their partnership promises to become realities, their respective practice partners have to, generally, take a pay cut; meaning, if you are commanding an equitable share of the aggregate profit margin, you are diluting the percentage going into their pockets. With this stated, you need to ensure that your contract reflects the partnership opportunity within a defined timeframe (essentially that it is automatic), and eliminate any language that preempts and/or supersedes the covenant. Look out for language like what follows:

> *You comprehend and acknowledge that there are numerous unforeseen scenarios that could impact the practice setting and, therefore, you understand and agree that the intention of the existing Practice leadership to make you an equitable partner within a three-year timeframe is not construed or inferred to be an enforceable commitment or binding in any manner or within any timeframe.*

If you are in good standing with the practice, all non-binding verbiage as it applies to your partnership opportunity should be eliminated. Additionally, do not sign the contract unless your ability to seamlessly transition into a partnership/equitable ownership position within the practice is clearly defined within the language. Lastly, if you have to purchase into your partnership, you need to make sure that you are only purchasing the tangible assets of the practice at their depreciated value—you should not have to extend capital for good will, future volumes, a patient base, or sweat equity. For example. To ensure you understand the equitable share you're buying, before signing your contract, you need to request an evaluation of the practice and have it attached as an addendum to your contract with language that specifies it as the agreed-upon method to determine your "buy in" price. In three years, you can use the addendum as a benchmark to contrast the new evaluation/buy-in price against.

Time off (vacation, sick, holiday, and professional development)

Vacation, sick, holiday, and professional development time, whether allotted or accrued, should be spelled out within your contract, and you should know and have language detailing whether or not you are allowed to carry forward unused time. Also, will you be reimbursed for unused time upon separation? Are there any unwritten or unknown restrictive covenants placed upon use of time off?

For example, I worked for an institution that provided annually, by contract, five days and up to $3,000 for external continuing medical education (CME) credits/professional development. Nevertheless, there was an unwritten policy stating that the money could only be used for CME events within the continental United States, and if a physician wasn't told this during recruitment (or if the physician didn't remember), it was determined when the travel and time-off requests were denied. Additionally, you don't want to take a vacation week you assumed carried forward from the previous year only to find out that you exhausted your vacation time for the current year. The time-off benefits outlined during your recruitment should be reflected in your contract or, at the very least, a benefits summary should be attached as an addendum.

Case Study 8
Recruitment scenario

Hospitalist position (full-time) in the Midwest, $200,000 per year.

- Employment Model: Private practice
- Compensation Model: Salaried
- Market Potential: Excellent
- Call Coverage: N/A

The hospitalist was recruited with the promise that she would become a full partner after three years of service to the group.

Reality

Two of the three partners left the practice, and the remaining partner negotiated a lucrative contract with a local hospital to provide hospitalist services. A few months later, the hospitalist achieved three years of tenure with the practice and assumed that the remaining partner would schedule a meeting to discuss her opportunity to become a full partner. The hospitalist waited months for the call that never came before requesting a meeting. At the meeting, the partner let her know that her agreement was with his previous partners, not with him, and that he was not obligated to make her a partner and/or increase her compensation to that of a partner. The hospitalist was furious and upon review of her employment contract was disheartened to find that her recruitment discussions of becoming a partner were not reflected within document she had executed. The hospitalist hired a lawyer and attempted to go down the breach-of-contract path, based on discussions that took place during her recruitment. Unfortunately, it was all for not, and to add insult to injury, she had a stressed professional relationship with the remaining partner, and she had to pay for her attorney's fees. Angry and feeling betrayed, she began looking for other professional opportunities, and I had an chance to interview her months after the situation had culminated. Although I was recruiting for a hospitalist provider, and my hospital was incurring a significant financial burden because we were staffing through a locums agency, I could not extend an employment offer. Why? It was because the hospitalist was still outwardly angry and hostile, and my team was afraid that she would be disruptive.

Chapter 14

Interviewing Checklist

- [✔] **Compensation** _____

- [✔] **Employment model**

    Employed _____

    Productivity

    Net Revenue _____

    Income Guarantee _____

- [✔] **Benefits**

    Insurances (health, dental, vision, and disability)

    _____

    Retirement

    _____

    Earned time off (vacation, sick, holiday, and professional development)

    _____

- [✔] **Other financial benefits**

    Relocation allowance _____

    Sign-on bonus _____

    Tuition reimbursement _____

    Other _____

- [✔] **Malpractice insurance (per occurrence or claims made?)**

    Tail insurance coverage _____

PHYSICIAN'S GUIDE: EVALUATING EMPLOYMENT OPPORTUNITIES
AND AVOIDING CONTRACTUAL PITFALLS

- [✔] **Patient volume**

    Market assessment   _____

    Pro forma   _____

    Request Copies

- [✔] **Call expectations**

    Emergency department   _____

    Practice   _____

    Telephone/Other   _____

- [✔] **Equipment and resources**

    _____

    _____

    _____

- [✔] **Initial cultural assessment**

    Physician satisfaction   _____

    Nursing/employee satisfaction   _____

    Patient satisfaction   _____

    Quality of care   _____

    Financial health   _____

    Name and contact number of predecessor   _____

    Request Copies

✔ Governance

    Medical staff bylaws

    Rules and regulations of the medical staff

    Employment policies

    Request Copies

✔ Recruitment promises

- _____

- _____

- _____

- _____

- _____

Contrast your interviewing checklist against your contract.

Chapter 15
Contracting Checklist

☑ **Recruitment promises**

- Make sure all recruitment promises are reflected in your contract (including partnerships).

☑ **Contract term**

- Evergreen versus a defined time period, make sure that COLA increases are reflected within your contract.

☑ **Compensation**

- Use granular, easily interpreted language, and eliminate any language allowing your employer to reduce your salary.

☑ **Employment model**

- If patient volumes have not been identified, transfer the financial burden from you to your employer by requesting and contracting for an employed employment model.

☑ **Benefits**

- All benefits should be referenced within the contractual language, and the list of benefits (or benefit options) should be attached to your contract as an addendum.

☑ **Malpractice insurance**

- Make sure the contract states that the employer will cover the cost of the malpractice insurance and that it specifies the type of coverage (per occurrence or claims made). If it is a claims-made policy, make sure the contract reflects that the cost of the tail will be assumed by your employer, and that the employer must provide you with tail coverage (versus leaving you bare).

☑ **Call expectations**

- Make sure all call expectations (emergency department, practice, and so forth) are spelled out in your contract.
    - Replace all "equitable" share language with "not to exceed."
    - If you are providing more than one type of call, to reduce the frequency, add "concurrent" language, which allows you to provide both call rotations contemporaneously.

PHYSICIAN'S GUIDE: EVALUATING EMPLOYMENT OPPORTUNITIES
AND AVOIDING CONTRACTUAL PITFALLS

- [✔] **Moving allowance**

  - Make sure your moving allowance is contractually obligated, and remove any language calling for you to pay back and/or have the expense forgiven over time (it is a reasonable and customary part of doing business).

- [✔] **Upfront money (tuition reimbursement, sign-on bonus, etc.)**

  - Reverse engineer the forgiveness over time by using tenure as a mechanism to trigger tuition reimbursement.

    Example language: For each year worked, Physician will receive $10,000 in tuition reimbursement that will be paid within thirty (30) days of the Physician's anniversary of the date that he/she commenced his/her practice within the medical community. If the Physician leaves or is no longer employed by Employer, for any reason other than termination for cause, the Employer will pay a prorated share of the tuition reimbursement prior to the physician's last date of employment.

  - If you decide it is in your best interest to take the money upfront, make sure the forgiveness schedule matches the length of the contract.

- [✔] **Termination covenants**

  - Termination without cause—delete this covenant.
    - If you cannot delete it, build the 90/180 rule into the contract (you provide 90 days notice, and your employer provides you with 180 days).
    - If you provide notice, make sure your employer cannot terminate you and/or have you stop work before your notice period.

  - Termination of practice location.
    - Apply the 180-day notice rule and the right to fill any applicable vacant position for which your employer is recruiting.

  - Termination for cause (breach).
    - Make sure you paid and provided benefits during the "cure" period.
    - Make sure you are not responsible for employer legal fees.

- [✔] **Non-Compete Covenants**

  - Delete, if possible, and if not, then you need to ensure the two defining factors of distance and time are included.
    - Distance should be the lesser of the defined primary service area or 25 miles.
    - Time should not last longer than two years.

- If your spouse is in a related medical profession, make sure the language does not affect the ability to secure employment with a "competitor."

- Make sure that the non-compete is null and void under the following scenarios:

    - Your employer terminates you without cause.
    - Your employing entity is sold, merged, and/or declares bankruptcy.
    - Upon the mutual written agreement.

✔ Equipment

- Make sure your equipment needs are reflected within the wording of the contract, referencing an equipment list by vendor, which is attached to the contract as an addendum. The contract or the addendum should reference the purchase timeframe.

Epilogue

The more I talked to residents and early careerists while penning this guide, the more convinced I became that it was a necessity to write this, have it published, and make it accessible to physicians who are in the early stages of their careers. From the random e-mail from a physician in the Southeast who stated that he had attended the best schools in the country and still didn't know how to effectively select and contract for employment to a resident who attended one of my grand rounds lectures expressing concern that I may not be available to advise him when he is ready to contract for his first position, I've been increasingly, if not accidentally, encouraged to finish this guide.

Does this guide cover every nuance you might read within your employment contract? It does not. However, it does provide insight and case study examples of the common contractual pitfalls I've personally witnessed for the better part of 20 years. For all other contractual covenants that are not easily interpreted, be sure to ask questions and provide the responses to the individual who is assisting you with negotiating the terms. Don't go it alone, and don't accept the default line, "This is our standard contract." It may very well be the standard template; however, if it doesn't represent your best interests, then revise it! If your potential employers are unwilling to revise the contract to represent the best interests of their entity and you, then you have to make a difficult determination: Do you want to work for inflexible employers? The telltale sign of a good negotiation is that neither party is happy (after meeting in the middle), but both parties feel respected.

Remember, recruitment is like being courted and the contract, essentially, is your prenuptial agreement. With this stated, the time to ensure that your interests are protected is when the relationship is strong, not when it begins to deteriorate.

How successful would you be negotiating a prenuptial agreement after you're married, or worse, in the midst of divorce? Point made.

Finally, always remember to get representation when negotiating your contract from an individual familiar with employment contracts and the complexities of the healthcare industry to ensure the spirit of your agreement is captured and to protect yourself from the unwanted professional and personal disruptions experienced by some of the physicians I've met during my career. You are a scarce commodity, and I firmly believe that you can negotiate a contract that balances the delicate ecology that exists between professional satisfaction and personal happiness.

Good luck.

About the Author

Thomas C. Crawford, MBA, FACHE, is a seasoned senior healthcare executive who has consistently delivered strategic level accomplishments within physician networks, hospitals, medical centers, and within an alliance framework. Additionally, his track record of success includes developing system-wide initiatives that have contributed to organizational effectiveness, bottom-line profitability, and growth; enhanced the quality and safety of the care delivered; and improved physician, clinician, and employee morale.

Thomas is currently serving as a member of the Faculty at a prominent Southeastern university. Thomas lives in Northern Florida, with his wife Carrie and sons, Jacob and Nathan.

References

Bagley, C.E. (2002). *Managers and the legal environment: Strategies for the 21st century* (4th edition). Cincinnati, OH: West Legal Studies in Business, a division of Thomson Learning.

Cejka Search. (2009). Retrieved from http://www.cejkasearch.com/Physician-Retention-Survey/2006RetentionSurvey/default.htm

Culture. (2010). In *Dictionary.com.* Retrieved from http://dictionary.reference.com/browse/culture

Dill, M.J. & Salsberg, E.S. (2008). *The Complexities of Physician Supply and Demand: Projections Through 2025*. Washington, D.C.: Association of American Medical Colleges.

HRSA Shortage Designation: HPSAs, MUAs & MUPs. (2010). Retrieved from http://bhpr.hrsa.gov/shortage/

Pro Forma. (2010). In *Dictionary.com.* Retrieved from http://dictionary.reference.com/browse/pro+forma

Review of Physician Recruiting Incentives (2010). Merritt Hawkins an AMN Healthcare Company. Retrieved from http://www.merritthawkins.com/compensation-surveys.aspx

CPSIA information can be obtained
at www.ICGtesting.com
Printed in the USA
LVIC04n0314071014
407546LV00002B/3